Ken Hathaway comes from a family of clerics, with his father and two brothers also being ministers. Following his training for the ministry, he served for a number of years in a country parish before taking up a teaching post in a minor public school, where he became head of the department, sixth form tutor and deputy head. He was also invited to act as an examiner at A levels by the Oxford local exam board, before developing his interests in business, whilst still continuing his ministry. He has also published a number of articles and edited a youth magazine. This book is the product of his years in teaching and ministry in which he came to recognise the need for a greater understanding of the Bible and its relevance to modern society.

In memory of my father, Rev W.G. Hathaway, to whom I owe so much.

In grateful thanks to my wife, Julien, for her patient love and understanding.

Ken Hathaway

THE CHILDREN OF GOD

AUSTIN MACAULEY PUBLISHERS®

LONDON * CAMBRIDGE * NEW YORK * SHARJAH

Except where otherwise stated all scripture quotations are from the Good News Bible published by The Bible Societies/Collins C American Bible Society.

A CIP catalogue record for this title is available from the British Library.

ISBN 9781035897476 (Paperback)
ISBN 9781035897483 (ePub e-book)

www.austinmacauley.com

First Published 2025
Austin Macauley Publishers Ltd®
1 Canada Square
Canary Wharf
London
E14 5AA

Table of Contents

And there's another country I've heard of long ago,
Most dear to them that love her, Most great to them that know;
We may not count her armies, We may not see her King;
Her fortress is a faithful heart, her pride is suffering;
And soul by soul and silently, Her shining bounds increase,
And her ways are ways of gentleness, and all her paths are peace.
Cecil Spring-Rice.

Introduction

What relevance does the book known as The Bible have for anyone in the 21st century? This is becoming an increasing issue for the modern generation, which is addicted to the smartphone and finds it difficult to read anything of length. In the same way, we are often told that religion, especially Christianity for the Western world, has little or no relevance in these modern times and can be relegated to a past age, being seen as a relic of a more superstitious and technically ignorant time, a period in which the vast volume of the 'unknown' was simply seen as fantasy. Which was often linked to the idea that the effects upon this planet and its occupants were caused by other celestial bodies. Not based on any proven science.

In more recent times, there has been a dramatic increase in general scientific understanding, now freely available through the internet and the mass media. It is recorded that Professor Stephen Hawking, the eminent scientist who suffered so severely from motor neuron disease, was once asked whether he believed in God. In his answer, which was only made possible by a very ingenious electronic machine, he said that he believed in 'facts' and that science provided these facts, whereas a belief in God did not. He stated that for many years he had believed that his disease was a 'curse from God' until he came to believe that science proved that this kind of God did not exist. The universe was not created, which implied a creator and a purpose. "No," he said, "there is no God, and therefore there is no existence after death."

What Stephen Hawking's reply suggests is that his illness, if not a direct act of a 'god', was the result of another factor, namely that humans are subject to other damaging forces in nature, such as illness, or sheer 'bad luck', or being in the wrong place at the wrong time. The idea that there are both good forces and evil or damaging forces in the universe was accepted in their day by the Greek philosophers, who tried to understand these forces, which they often attributed to actions of the goddess 'Fortuna'. The basic question they were asking was,

'Why should the good man suffer?' However, the two major Greek philosophers of the period differed in their approach to finding the answers to such questions.

Aristotle, who was a marine biologist, believed that to find the answer to any problem, one must examine the physical evidence, and from that, one can deduce the answers. On the other hand, Plato, a student of Socrates, believed that the world, the universe, was immaterial; therefore, the answers must be found by thought, through the mind, discourse, and discussion. Hence, the so-called Socratic Dialogue, through which, by asking the right questions, they believed that one would eventually arrive at the correct answer.

In the Bible, the idea of both an external evil force acting on humanity and the presence of good supernatural forces is recognized repeatedly. It begins with the creation story in which Adam and Eve are depicted as perfect beings in close communion with their creator, God, able to converse with Him, but also being subject to other forces, symbolized by the snake, which were able to corrupt the perfect beings by attacking their mind, the thought process. So, in the Genesis account, Eve succumbs to the offer of ultimate knowledge made by the 'snake', unaware that through the possession of superior knowledge comes the loss of innocence, just as in these days is happening to young people through the 'mass media'. In the case of Eve, this also involved a death, which was the loss of her spiritual life. It is these factors present in the text which give the first part of Genesis its symbolic value, enabling future readers to analyse the ongoing situation and relate it to our modern day by careful thought, as well as providing illustrative evidence. In fact, if one is prepared to accept that many facets of the Bible were intended to be read symbolically, much of what might seem implausible suddenly becomes not only more acceptable but also far more interesting for those who read it. Therefore, we need to be aware that Christianity is not just about the personal well-being of 'believers'; it is also about the purpose which underlies the whole of creation.

For that reason, we must not regard the Bible purely in terms of the past. A very careful study of the Bible can also provide answers to questions about the present and the future, rather than simply exploring the past, which science, with all the infinite resources available to it, has been unable to do. Questions such as, if this is a created universe rather than a scientific accident, then what is God's plan for the future, both of mankind and this vast, rapidly expanding universe? What is the purpose which underlies creation? Does it have a future, or will it progressively end so that newly evolving systems will replace what we now know, just as past civilisations, newly discovered, reveal a surprisingly capable past which then simply ceased to exist? Even more startling, can the Bible provide any answer to the biggest question of all: are we alone? Is there recognisable life elsewhere in this vast space around us?

Chapter 1
Symbolism

That there are in the Bible a number of incidents which can be read symbolically, as representative of ideas or principles, as well as being literally true, has long been understood. And in that case, the symbolic representation speaks on two levels. It can be used both to define a simple, recognisable and relevant situation, which might involve an individual or a community, but it can also be developed on a national and, potentially, on an international level, with profound implications also for the future, but which is concealed from the unwary or careless reader. Which then lifts the incident from being mundane or even implausible until it becomes the presentation of an eternal world truth, which was developing here on earth, but one which it was not possible to understand physically at the time. Such is in fact the whole book of Revelation, written as it was in a kind of code, probably understood by its readers at the time but deliberately hidden to avoid causing offence to the authorities who had imprisoned John. Hence the supernatural element, the Divine representation of angels and visions, was only available to a person, like John, who had been spiritually very close to Jesus during His life and whose relationship, developed in isolation on the Island of Patmos, was now even closer. It is this concept, of an underlying deeper perception, which irradiates the early pages of the Bible as we read it. Thus creating for the modern reader of the Bible its enduring and never-ending challenge and inspiration. And it is this element which puts it firmly in the realm of relevance to modern everyday life.

For example, in the Old Testament, we have the presence of heavenly beings and visions and other great events, which become representative of eternal truths, becoming one way of expressing or interpreting what otherwise would be ideas and facts inexplicable at the time. Just as in the New Testament, Jesus taught the crowds in parables. Which was a method of presenting sublime truth in a way which could be understood by the hearers through the use of commonplace symbols and word pictures which illustrated difficult eternal truths in a way which was readily understandable.

If we take the Biblical account in Genesis literally, the story of Adam and Eve might simply serve to warn her children, her descendants, to be careful of snakes, because any encounter will be a painful experience for the child. If, instead, we read this as a symbolic statement, then when we look back, we can see that the story was predicting an encounter between a human being, Eve's descendant, challenging and defeating an enemy but being hurt in the process. In other words, this was a very early expression of the Jewish hope of a deliverer who would set their nation free. Which was enacted, some four thousand years later, in the life and death of Jesus. Crucified by evil forces but resurrected by God to redeem mankind from evil. So that the one whom they had rejected became the underlying element of what we now call Christianity, the deliverance of humankind from the power of evil, which ultimately is death, and offering an eternal life to all who believe it.

Jesus, who was one of Eve's descendants, would, during His time on earth, encounter the evil forces which, in this case, were represented not by the occupying Roman authorities but more poignantly by errant forces existing within His own people. Who, in ignorance, had killed the one who came to deliver them. The jealousy, pride, ambition, and a desire to be popular, particularly amongst the religious leaders, challenged the authority and laws of God, as expressed in His Covenant. An agreement made first with Adam and Eve, then later with Noah, in much greater detail with Abraham, and then finally with Moses on Mt. Sinai.

A clear example of this evil force is seen in the actions of the leading Jews of our Lord's day. Pilate, the Roman governor, wanted to release Jesus, stating that he found no fault in Him, but the Jewish religious leaders wanted to kill Him to get rid of Him, and in order to do so they disguised their actions as being political expediency to avoid conflict with their Roman overlords, to whom the Jewish religious ideas were of no importance. Realistically, however, their actions were motivated largely by jealousy, a fact which both Pilate and Herod clearly recognized. But the religious leaders also saw Him as a threat to their status, their standing in society, because He had been very critical of their hypocrisy, their false standards, and their corruption of their God-given role as leaders of that community. However, to complete the relevance of the symbolism in Genesis, Jesus would then be vindicated by His father God, who simply raised Him to life again three days later, thereby overturning the action of the 'snake' in killing Him. Hence the 'snake's' head was destroyed, but the child only suffered a 'bruised heel'. The snake in this case symbolically representing the evil principle which was opposing God. The 'external force' which we have mentioned.

No wonder that Paul, writing later, would say that we "wrestle not against flesh and blood but against principalities, against powers, against the rulers of the darkness of this world, against wickedness in high places." Ephesians 6:12. Which, for the time it was written, was a very challenging and illuminating statement.

Jesus refers to this same factor, of an external contrary force, in his symbolic story about the farmer who sowed good seed in his field, but during the night an enemy came and sowed tares amongst the wheat. His workers wanted to uproot them, but Jesus said, "No, lest in uprooting the weeds you damage the good seeds." Matthew 13: 24–30 a.v. Interestingly, the 'tares' mentioned were a poisonous plant which resembled wheat until it was fully grown, therefore difficult to distinguish from the good seed until they were both mature. In other words, in nature there are things which are potentially bad and harmful. Nature itself and humans can suffer adverse effects, which cause great suffering and pain. This is illustrated for us in the book of Job, whether literally true or there as a parable, which begins by telling of a good man who had no faults yet suffered immeasurably because of external forces, not caused by him, which destroyed his family and all his wealth. In this case, the external forces are represented by Satan, who was allowed to challenge Job's belief and faith in God. Even his friends were convinced that Job was being punished by God, and his wife told him to commit suicide. Yet he maintains throughout that he was innocent of any known fault. Satan in this parable being symbolic of those forces of nature which may cause us harm or personal injury. See the book of Job.

In response to this story, we are bound to ask, "Why did the innocent good man suffer?" Just as the ancient Greeks questioned in their philosophical writings, they portrayed the evil forces as being personified in the goddess Fortuna. Their illustration of the way this affected people was to imply that humanity is strapped to 'Ixion's wheel', which, as it rotates, causes the fortunes of man to rise and fall, irrespective of the man's own activities or his character. In the account of Job and other incidents, the Bible is exploring these major

15

issues from the very earliest times, and for this reason alone, we can say that the substance of the book was and still is relevant to the human condition.

Those who believe in God are convinced, as Paul will later state, that ultimately "All things work together for good, to them that love God, to those who are called according to His purpose." Romans 8:28. In other words, there is an underlying purpose in creation, and that ultimately, because God is in control, even acts directed by the evil forces cannot break our relationship with this God, and that, by His mercy, even those unfortunate events will ultimately produce goodness if we can trust God. Neither life nor death nor any other creature can separate us from the love of God. But that does not explain why these things happen, why otherwise 'good' people experience problems when often the 'bad' people live happily, and for that answer we shall look further into what the scriptures say.

Christians believe that whilst our contact with God ultimately is an act of faith, which is described by Paul as being "the substance of things hoped for, the evidence of things not seen." Hebrews 11:1 The physical evidence for His existence is available to anyone who seeks Him, and true faith can bring us into an understanding of the 'why' of creation, which is revealed frequently through the symbolism as well as being directly stated. Indeed, the whole issue of what the French call the 'raison etre', the whole point of existence, becomes available to the astute reader. As is the wider issue of whether the existence of the universe and everything in it has any purpose, as opposed to being totally random. Much of that 'evidence' is to be found in the Bible, in its record of God's engagement with humanity. What this book seeks to do is to look at that evidence, most particularly in the lives of people.

For many people today the big question is, "Why should I or anyone in the twenty-first century read the Bible? It is out of date and does not reflect the values of our modern society." The fact is that whilst the values of our modern society may have changed, along with all the modern electronic appurtenances of our daily lives which have made life physically easier, the result has been that people today face challenges which were not even contemplated years ago, and these challenges are putting people, especially young people, under enormous pressure. As is happening through their exposure to the 'mass media'. However, we cannot avoid the conclusion that 'evil' does exist, especially evident in the otherwise inexplicable actions of some people. Most particularly in those who, through these modern devices, have the greatest potential to affect the lives of others. At the lowest level, the worst of these pressures may be mainly those connected with self-esteem and the need to conform to almost impossible standards set by the so-called 'influencers', whose lives are capable of having a good or bad effect on others. At an international level, such forces destroy nations and cause inexpressible suffering.

People's sense of values, things that are important, have changed our way of life so dramatically, especially in the last fifty years. These changes have also come so rapidly, with greater changes occurring in the last hundred years than in all the many centuries of life before that. But with it, the problems faced by people today are also far greater, and the pressures on individuals are often more than many people can bear, particularly in the more highly developed societies. Some countries still have a far simpler and less complex social structure, but even there, human suffering, the problems of illness and disease, and the need to provide for a family are still present and, in so many cases, present insurmountable problems.

It is a fact that, in many cases, even though it may not be recognized, Christianity has done more than anything else over the years to form and shape our society. It was the early Christian missionaries who introduced the discipline of education and promoted learning in our country and elsewhere. They brought compassionate help to the poor and, through the principles introduced in the Old Testament and renewed in a loving and sympathetic way by the teaching and miracles of Jesus, they introduced the principles which underlie our laws and our social contacts. Introducing the concept of love and generosity, of humility and of personal sacrifice, into society. Christianity stands opposed to pride and self-service, to the love of wealth and prestige. God offers love and security and stability in a time of insecurity, and He offers eternal satisfaction and peace of mind to those who are prepared to believe in Him and accept His offer of forgiveness and love. And in turn, He enables people to live their lives in service to others. The Christian message also brings comfort to the lonely, the oppressed, and the underprivileged. Most of our national institutions were founded by Christian believers. The schools, the hospitals, and the social welfare communities came into being through Christian institutions. Further, Christianity answers most of the questions which we can ask about the nature of our world and the purpose behind it and offers certainty and security in a very unsettled and rapidly changing world, and it offers hope beyond the grave. Therefore, it can be a force for good in this life, as well as in offering the potential of a future existence free from all problems.

Most of world history is concerned with major political and military events and, in most cases, is written from the viewpoint of the victor. We rarely get to share the personal experiences of the ordinary folk involved, but they are the ones who are affected by what their rulers and leaders do. For those more personal, more intimate details, we have to turn to the writings of the poets and scribes, to the 'great' novelists, men like Charles Dickens, whose novels are focused on the social problems of his day and reflect the concerns recorded in the newspapers. Or of the women writers, such as Jane Austen or George Eliot (Mary Anne Evans). One great value of the Bible is that it also illustrates and emphasizes truths from the lives of individuals. Highlighting the love of God and the immeasurable blessing which He can bring and the dangers of ignoring His precepts through the lives of ordinary people. It illuminates history by describing the problems of humanity, ordinary people, from the earliest times, looking at the causes of human behaviour and the consequences of ignoring the basic facts. But of even greater significance, it introduces mankind to the creator as one who is loving, kind, and supportive of those who respond to Him and warns of impending doom, of judgement, for those who deny, ignore, or refuse to listen and obey. The great issue of the nation of Israel was that they forgot, or ignored, the lessons of the past. When they came to conquer the land of Canaan, forty years later after their deliverance from Egypt, they forgot the miraculous power by which God had delivered them from the grip of the great and powerful nation of Egypt. When they sinned, they forgot the severity of God's punishment. As occurred in the death of Aaron's two sons, Nadab and Abihu, Leviticus 10:1, because as priests they had ignored the holiness of God. A God who had appeared only as a fire on a mountain which became so holy that even to touch it meant death. Whose requirement was a daily offering of sacrifice for sin. Then we have Achan's sin of theft from Jericho which meant defeat for their army (Joshua chapter 7) and his death and that of his family. Or Miriam's rebellion, which resulted in leprosy, and the death of 250 people through the rebellion of Korah, Dathan, and Abiram and their followers, Numbers chapter 16. Time and time again, sin was severely punished.

Historically there are two things which probably best illustrate the positive values introduced by Christian faith. The first of these is the social, political, and religious consequences of the so-called conversion of the Roman Emperor

Constantine, which occurred because of a vision which he claimed to have seen at the time of the Battle of Milvian Bridge in 312, which gave him the supremacy of the Western half of the dying Roman Empire, which had been split into two, East and West. The night before the battle, he had seen in a dream a sign of a Cross-in the sky and heard a voice telling him to conquer under this sign. Already very tolerant to religious ideas, he claimed that after this he was a convert to Christianity. His Edict of Milan in 313 provided tolerance for the new Christian religion in the Roman Empire, which had previously persecuted followers of Jesus and even thrown them to lions in the Coliseum in Rome for the amusement of the populace, and it was this conjunction of church and state which enabled this 'new' religion to grow, expand, and become an increasing influence in society in general and also in terms of government acceptance of its basic principles. But, as we shall later see, it also marks the beginning of the politicalization of the Christian faith, which created problems for the teachings of Jesus of Nazareth.

This so-called 'conversion' of Constantine led to his calling a Conference of religious leaders in Nicaea in 325, at which the basic creed, which would define the Christian Church for centuries, was agreed upon and subsequently became known as the Nicaean Creed. He would later turn the old city of Byzantium into his capital, renaming it Constantinople, which we know as modern Istanbul. However, what concerns us is that his decision made Christianity the official religion of the Roman Empire. A decision which gave Christianity its world-reaching outlook and brought it to the forefront of all those nations which were under the dominion of the Roman Empire, and it also stopped the persecution of its believers.

Later, with the final collapse of the old Roman Empire in the fifth century, the Christian Church would retain much of the political status of the old Empire. Particularly in Italy, where the Vatican City was established in 590 by Pope Gregory. The Roman Church claims its absolute right of authority, and its commencement, to the presence of Peter in the city and the claim that Peter had been given a specific role by Christ, who gave him the 'keys to the Kingdom', Matthew 16:18–19 A.V. However, historically there is nothing to connect Peter with Rome. In fact, biblically it was Paul who ended up in Rome, albeit as a prisoner. There is no mention of Peter ever visiting the city.

What one can deduct from this and from historical records is that from the 6th Century onwards, the Church in Rome claimed both political and religious supremacy over the rapidly growing Christian belief and, in fact, the Pope became the first 'monarchical' head of state, and by means of its missionaries and the establishing of 'Roman' churches throughout Europe, it became a force to be reckoned with politically. Claiming, as it did, the sole right to determine man's spiritual destiny, it became a defining force in a world dominated by superstition, amongst people who were, in the main, both illiterate and uneducated, though not necessarily unintelligent.

The universal result of this was that the Church became a defining authority in a very superstitious age by being able to control events and claim to control the eternal destiny of men's souls. This may be a devious route, but effectively it worked for some good in society, although ultimately, one could claim that the Church lost its primary motive and then its reason for its existence by becoming not just the channel of God's message to humanity but the focus of worship. The new Roman hierarchy itself became the reason for its existence. However, its presence in a tumultuous and violent world in which the sword was the ultimate judge did have a profound effect in championing the rights of the individual against the 'might is right' philosophy of the powerful forces of the day, to whom the majority were mere numbers, not valuable individual characters.

Where the Medieval Church potentially lost out was in the fact that it became very wealthy and above criticism, largely through its claims to have God's sole authority over heaven and hell, which inspired donations and gifts given by the landed aristocracy in the belief that they could buy their way out of purgatory, receive forgiveness, and inherit the eternal blessings of God. This then led to landed families seeing the Church as a suitable occupation for younger sons, not as a Divine calling, when the eldest sons of the families were being prepared to inherit the families' estates, which often required allegiance to or service for the King. The younger sons then would enter the Church, where preferment and potential wealth were in the gift of the patrons of the Church diocese or parish, or on occasion, of the King himself, and not out of a sense of vocation. And many of the king's ministers of state were drawn from this source. It also resulted in a division within the Church's hierarchy between the educated offspring of those high in society, who had no spiritual aspirations, and the, often very poor, parish priests and clerks in holy office who had a vocation. Many of the latter were poorly educated. It was not uncommon for these to be semi-literate, well-meaning men whose knowledge of the Church's main medium of communication, Latin, was limited to their being able to repeat the liturgy from memory, and therefore they had no access to the niceties of spiritual knowledge, and because the then extant Bible was Jerome's Latin Vulgate, the ordinary people had no access to the source of truth. They were totally dependent on what their priest told them.

A further problem, which would later be highlighted by the German Monk, Martin Luther when he nailed his academic challenge over the sale of indulgences to the doors of the Church in Württemberg in 1514. The fact was that 'religion' had become a saleable commodity. Salvation was quantified, satisfied, in the number of prayers or masses said for their salvation, which had to be paid for, rather than in the true devotion and penance of the supplicant. Consequently, the role of the Church became increasingly influential and even defining politically. Resulting in the direction of the nation's affairs being frequently dictated by the Church in Rome more than by the King or the local aristocracy, which led in the 16th Century, to the collision between the King, Henry VIII, and the Pope, which was only resolved when the king finally rejected the Pope's authority and made himself the head of the Church in England. A role which the Monarch still holds today in our modern society and which is publicly acknowledged in the anointing of the Monarch at their coronation.

However, what is so important in this respect is that over one hundred years earlier, during the reign of Edward III, the nation had become increasingly concerned and disillusioned by the fact that so much of the nation's wealth was going to support a Papacy, which at the time was based in France. Then, towards the end of the 14th century, John Wycliffe, a former Master of Balliol College in Oxford, which, at the time, ranked with Paris as the foremost seat of learning in Europe, had become outspoken against the wealth and excesses of the Roman Church. For example, he spoke and wrote against the sale of 'indulgences', a legal religious sanction which enabled a person to purchase forgiveness for a crime before the crime had been committed. He based his views on a comparison with the life and the teaching of Jesus Christ, as expressed in the scriptures. He went on to criticise the worship of images as distracting from the worship of God, the sale of relics, and even the right to grant forgiveness of sin in return for payment and the Church's claim to have the sole right of entry into the Kingdom of God, usually in return for payment of some kind, which he saw was Rome's heretical way of financing its excessive wealth. And its political advances, such as the Crusades against the Turkish (Muslim) forces which were occupying the 'Holy Land'.

Wycliffe went even further by stating that the Word of God, as expressed in the holy scriptures, was the only source of religious truth, not the pronunciations of the Pope or the ecclesiastical hierarchy, whether in Rome or Avignon, and he stated that the scriptures were the only source of truth about God and His Church and the only true way to God and therefore should be available to every person in their own language and that they individually should be free to interpret the faith. All of which would undermine the so-called 'authority' of the Church. He also attacked the principal doctrines of the Church, including transubstantiation, in which, at the word of an 'ignorant' priest, the bread and wine of Holy Communion became the actual body and blood of Christ. Until his death in 1384, he spent his time translating the scriptures into English, but his message continued to be preached after his death in towns and cities in England and was also carried into Europe, where it was welcomed by many, such as the Hussite martyrs. In many ways Wycliffe's teachings and translations of the Bible were the precursors of the work which would begin one hundred years later with Martin Luther and which was further facilitated by the invention of printing by Gutenberg in Germany. The ability to print multiple copies made the work of the Reformers so readily available to the newly educated, who were at this time benefitting from the classic revival of the Greek language with its philosophy and literature in what we call the Renaissance, which by this time was also spreading amongst the educated people in England, particularly in the universities.

The second effect is the very dramatic impact which Christianity made on the social and political life of England, especially in the years from 900 AD to the twelfth century and beyond. The evidence is that Christianity was firmly established in England as early as 300 AD because the English Church sent two bishops to the conference in Nicaea in 314 AD. Sadly, after the departure of the Romans in the fifth century and under the atheistic influences of the succeeding invaders from Scandinavia, the religious life of the country was in decline, which is why in the succeeding centuries the Popes sent a number of missionaries, such as St Augustine, to reinforce the work of the native Christian leaders, such as St Patrick. The Monasteries established by the roman missionaries would become centres of learning and of the preparation and copying of manuscripts, and by the extreme vigour and regulated simplicity of their 'office', they created a disciplined response to authority. Equally, their concern for the poor, the destitute, and the sick provided the basis of social welfare. For a much more detailed appraisal of the impact of those early Christians upon society, see Arthur Bryant's remarkably detailed description in his very informative book 'Set in a Silver Sea'.

Some years later, the right of the Pope in Rome to control events, both spiritual and political, in England, was challenged by our King, Henry VIII, because of his determination to divorce Anne Bolyn, who was now past child-bearing age, and remarry in the hope of begetting a male heir to replace his two daughters. Which, at the time, led to the United Kingdom becoming one of the leading nations in an increasingly Protestant world. But, politically, it also came as the culmination of the ongoing conflict between the state and the rights of the individual. So that politically England became the most enlightened nation in Europe. Especially in the contest between the rights of the individual to be judged by his peers, which had been developing over a long period, from the time of King Alfred through the 12th Century Magna Carta, which limited the King's power, to the reforms of Henry II and James I. Further, by adopting as its moral code the Ten Commandments given to Moses, the principles of morality and social conduct became part of English Law and to this day underline our community relationships. It transformed the old law of 'might is right', under which justice was often reduced to the result of armed conflict, to a situation where everyone was entitled to justice by trial by one's peers. Henry VIII by his action, had broken the absolute political power which the ancient Church had exercised over ordinary people.

What becomes unmistakable and very evident as we read it is the fact that in the Old Testament God is seen as closely involved with His world. He meets with Abraham and discusses what He is going to do with the city of Sodom. Genesis 18:16. He uses the prophet Elijah to declare three years of drought and then defeats the 450 prophets of Baal who were sponsored by King Ahab's wife, Jezebel. God not only delivered the nation of Israel from its 400 years of servitude in Egypt but also led the vast number of Israelites through the wilderness for 40 years, even though their forty-year journey had been caused by their failure to obey God's command to begin their occupation and conquest because they listened to the very negative report of ten of the twelve men sent to explore the country for forty days, Numbers 13:25–33, in spite of their very vivid memory of the way God had defeated the Egyptian army at the crossing of the Red Sea. Exodus chapter 14. And then guiding them with a pillar of fire at night and a cloud by day. He fed those Israelites for 40 years, during which time their clothes, even their shoes, did not wear out. God met personally with Hagar after her expulsion by Sarah, and He fought a spiritual battle with Jacob at Peniel before humbling him. He spoke to the young prophet Samuel and enabled Joseph to read dreams and become next in authority to the Pharoah himself. However, in the New Testament, after the Ascension of our Lord, His disciples were all given the power of the Holy Spirit, giving them all access to knowledge and understanding. This personal experience of knowing God became universally available to all believers. Joel 2:28.

At this point it must be recognized that the Old Testament and the New Testament are inextricably linked, and the nature of that link is vital to any understanding of the Bible. The Old Testament is an account of God's chosen race, the Jews, who trace their ancestry back to God's covenant with Abraham. By following his faith, the children of Abraham became 'God's children, who were the benefactors of the Covenant, with its obligations and its vast promises'. These promises were, under the terms of the Covenant, conditional upon their adhering to the terms of that Covenant. Any deviation from those terms would incur the wrath of the author, God Himself, and they were to be judged on their faithfulness to that Covenant, as in the Ten Commandments. Any deviation, such as the worship of other gods. Even the erecting of statues of saints and of Mary can become objects of veneration or worship. In the same way, prayers offered to saints or to Mary are contrary to the two statements, 'Thou shalt have no other gods' (Exodus 20:3–4) and 'There is only one mediator between us and God, the Lord Jesus Christ'. 1 Timothy 2:5. These were listed above the sins of theft, jealousy, and adultery. The whole of the Old Testament is related to God's children through Abraham and his son Isaac, not Ishmael the firstborn to a servant woman, and then it was Jacob, not the first born twin Esau, whose twelve sons became the twelve tribes of Israel. They were a chosen people.

What we have to understand is that the historical books of the Old Testament relate to events which had already happened by the time they were written and the prophetic books to events which were to be fulfilled at some time in the future. A good example is found in the prophetic book of Isaiah, where the promises to a deeply troubled nation of a king who would restore their nation to a greater glory and all the details of his birth and suffering referred, as we now know, to the coming of God's own Son Jesus Christ, whose rejection by them would lead to the most devastating events of the Roman occupation and destruction of Jerusalem in AD 70 and the subsequent removal of all its inhabitants. An event which was only overturned on 8th May 1948 when the state of Israel was reestablished and its native people were allowed to return after almost 2,000 years of exile. Which means that there are a lot of prophetic, future events still to occur.

The New Testament begins with the revelations of Jesus, which were subsequently picked up by the Apostles and disciples of Jesus and became the basis of what became known as Christianity. These revelations will refer to the 'secret' message, as Paul calls it, that with the demise of the Jewish nation, a new race of God's children would be chosen. A new race, born not of Abraham but of God by the Holy Spirit, as Jesus explained to Nikodemus in John 3:16, a race who would receive total forgiveness through the sacrifice of Jesus on the Cross, not subject to the old covenant nor judged for the sins of the Jewish race, who yet still have a unique relationship with God. Which means that the Jews, as described by Paul in his letters to Romans and Hebrews, have yet to face judgement. Which will happen when Jesus returns. At which point we are told, they will at last recognize in Him their promised King, Saviour, and Lord.

Now, one major link between the Old and the New Testaments is that events in the Old Testament can be seen symbolically to speak of events which occur in the New Testament. For example, the 'seed of the woman', Eve, is now seen to refer to the advent of Jesus Christ, whose death on the cross ended Satan's power over humanity, paid our debt, and set us free. His subsequent resurrection being not just God's vindication of His son but the promise of eternal life. Jesus refers to the raising of the serpent on a pole by Moses to deliver the children of Israel from the plague and refers to Himself. "As Moses lifted up the serpent in the wilderness, even so shall the Son of Man be lifted up, and all who look on Him shall be saved." The story of Noah and the Flood illustrates the creation of a new world order after a massive destruction.

A thorough search shows how, taken symbolically, so very many parts of the Old Testament are prefiguring the new order of the New Testament, as well as being relevant to the Jewish nation, as Peter says, 1 Peter 1:10–12. "It was concerning this salvation that the prophets made a careful search and investigation, and they prophesied about this gift which God would give you. They tried to find out when the time would be and how it would come." Which is why a study of the Old Testament can be so helpful in our understanding of the whole purpose of God, who had planned the whole thing from the very beginning, so that Paul, writing, could say that we "are chosen in Christ from before the beginning of the world." Ephesians 1:4. A.v.

All through the Old Testament, we find that events and prophecies have a relevance to the New Order. Paul makes much of the role of Jesus Christ as Saviour, High Priest and King, in his letter to Hebrews, trying to make the renegade Jews understand that Jesus is the final answer to their aspirations, their hopes.

We can also note that in the Old Testament, apart from selected individuals, God only dealt with His people through the mediation of a chosen few. Men like the priests and the prophets, and unfortunately, His people were often led by kings. Kings who were so often themselves bad leaders and caused the people to suffer. A classic case can be seen in the foolish actions of King Asa in 2 Chronicles 28: 1–8, where the nation saw 200,000 of the nation's women and children captured by the Northern kingdom of Israel. Whereas under the reforms of King Hezekiah the nation prospered.

In the New Testament every individual became responsible to God through His gift of the Holy Spirit, which had been promised to 'all flesh', as foretold in Joel 2:8 and occurred after the death, resurrection, and ascension of Jesus, as recorded in Acts chapter 2, and which made the wisdom and understanding of God available to everyone. As Jesus Himself had told His disciples in John 14 and 16. After this event, ordinary people were able to be guided by the Holy Spirit and also taught and empowered by Him. Further, as Jesus promised in John 14 and 16, God, through His Holy Spirit, gave to individual people 'gifts' of various abilities, such as teaching, preaching, and the ability to heal the sick. Paul the apostle would later point out that these gifts enable each dedicated individual to be empowered by God for every challenge. 1 Corinthians 12. In this respect the Church of today is sadly lacking, relying on human wisdom and knowledge. Whereas under the new regime it was 'not by might nor by power but by My Spirit', Zechariah 4:6, 'that the excellency of the power might be of God and not of man'. 2 Corinthians 4:7.

Sadly, the simple truth of the Gospel, as taught by Jesus and followed closely by those early disciples, has been progressively corrupted, so that today we find various 'creeds' and unorthodox beliefs, which either add ideas which have no justification in scripture or deny much of the authenticity of the Bible and of the faith passed down to us through the New Testament. For example, prayers directed to saints who have died and, more explicitly, the whole constructed veneration of Mary, which includes prayers directed to God through her and not through the 'priesthood of Jesus. A cult which involves the belief that she was born supernaturally and that she did not die but was received into heaven. All of which is not merely of human construction but has absolutely no basis in scripture and contradicts a number of statements made by Jesus, such as when Mary and Jesus' brothers and sisters come demanding to see Him, He rejects them with, "Who is my mother and brothers? But these disciples." Matthew 12:48.

There are so many other deviant versions of the Gospel, many sheltering behind elements of the truth. For example, the Mormon Church, which bases much of its belief on the so-called Book of Mormon, dictated to their founder, Joseph Smith, by an angel.

However, a total realignment of Christian faith, and one which replaced much of Catholic dogma with a simple 'act of faith', began in the 16th century as Martin Luther's message spread to England and the rest of Europe. Helped in so many ways by Henry VIII's rejection of the authority of the Pope when he became the head of the Church in England. But it took a further century before Parliamentary reform gave rise to such as the Act of Toleration in 1689, which authorized religious groups other than members of the Established Church to worship freely and removed the burden of compliance from other practicing Christians, such as the Congregational Church, the Presbyterians, the Baptists, and later the Methodists under the brothers Wesley, John and Charles, who were Oxford-educated, ordained ministers of the Anglican Church who took their preaching into the churchyards, the fields, and the streets after they were forbidden to preach in the Established Church buildings.

Their preaching and Charles' theologically important hymns led to a great revival of Christianity in the 18th century, and this was followed by a further series of evangelistic movements, culminating in the Welsh Revival of 1904, led by an inspired local man, Evan Roberts, which saw the spread of evangelical Christianity in Wales, and most recently, in the 1950s and 1960s, the major evangelistic crusades of Dr Billy Graham, who was entertained at Buckingham Palace by our late Queen, during one of his missions.

The remarkable thing about the Christian God is not just that He is declared to be the creator of all things which exist but that at the same time He is also a spiritual being and therefore unknown and unknowable to created beings. However, as we progress from the Old Testament to the New, we see a seismic change in our perception of God. He is no longer just seen in the symbolism of the burning bush or the fire at Mount Sinai, the mountain which could not be touched because the visitation was violent and destructive, but in the face of Jesus Christ, His son, we see a God who is sympathetic to our problems, is forgiving and encouraging, and does everything He can to help us in our understanding. Historically and genetically, early man was ignorant of anything which he could not see or feel. Even the forces of nature were seen as uncontrollable forces which one tried to placate, seeking by sacrifice and propitiation to appease them. Looking back, we marvel at the thing which those early people did, their achievements, in seeking to 'control' or regulate those unseen forces. The ancient monuments erected to appease the anger of the gods are remarkable monuments which demonstrate man's ingenuity and both physical and mental ability to the point that we are amazed that they accomplished so much. How did the Egyptians build the Giza pyramids with such precise mathematical accuracy and without access to mechanical devices? How did the inhabitants of Salisbury Plain over 3,000 years ago transport, erect, and align their stones with such accuracy to pinpoint midsummer and midwinter? Eventually their discoveries about the calculable order of the universe confirmed their primitive belief that there was order and discipline in, for example, the rising and decline of the sun and its seasons. And the existence of a regularity in the movement of stars and planets.

Christians accept that God is the source of everything which currently exists and everything which it is possible to exist, whilst science, by research into the very nature of things, seeks to find when and how the whole process began and what lies behind that. However, the 'primitive' mind perceived that this 'authority' or life-giving force might exist in several different forms. Hence, the mythology which grew around these ideas, which gave supernatural powers to these 'gods', attributing to them the emotions and the energies which they themselves understood as motivating forces.

Yet, to ordinary people at that time, the actual creator was unknowable. Not simply because their minds were unable to understand the complexity of creation but because He is a spiritual being; therefore, 'immortal and invisible', as the hymn writer Walter Chalmers Smith so adroitly puts it. Whilst the scripture simply states, "No man hath seen God. The only Son, who is the same as God and is at the Father's side, He has made Him known." John 1:18. What the Bible enables us to understand is that when the appropriate time came in the development of man's understanding, He, God, would make Himself known to His creation in His actions and by His dealings with humanity so that ultimately, He became recognisable as the epitome of goodness, holiness, truth, and love in the person of His Son Jesus Christ, who came, born of a woman, to tell us, "He that hath seen Me hath seen the Father. The Father and I are one." John 14:9. The God of the Bible, as the creator of the universe, is, ultimately, absolute power, authority, and utter purity, but at the same time, He is NOT a physical entity. Therefore, He cannot be represented in any man-made form. However, in order that mankind, which He had created, could get to know or understand the how and the why, God began to reveal himself to this humanity. First as the supreme authority who demands 'worship' and obedience, but then as one who has created everything for a purpose, and finally as one who is willing to help and succour a very limited humanity and enable it to achieve feats of intelligence, artistic ability, and love, as opposed to the negative aspects of which humanity was also capable, such as hatred, anger, and violence.

In revealing Himself to mankind through His Son Jesus and later through a 'converted' mankind, He has also demonstrated His power over the universe in acts of kindness and love, as well as in punishment, to demonstrate that all these things exist through a love which cannot be fully understood, that the humanity which had been created with limited ability and aspirations was destined to share the future with Him. For we are, "Chosen in Him from before the foundation of the world," Ephesians 1:4.

However, one principal fact that the Christian Gospel teaches is that to know this supernatural and spiritual God, one must have faith. One must believe that He exists and that He wants us to know Him, and that is why ultimately, He sent His 'Son', created supernaturally in the very form of created mankind, 'in all points like as we are'. And this remarkable event was to make two things evident. This person we know as Jesus was totally human. Which meant that the person we recognize as the son of God was made subject to all the limitations of the beings which He had created in order to understand fully and to deliver the beings which He had created from the weakness and failure to which it was prone. Sadly, all created humanity has "come short of the glory of God." Romans 3:23 av. We have failed to be what God wants us to be. Failed to achieve what is acceptable to Him but also failed to become what we are capable of. But this person, who was here to make God known, spoke with the authority of God and, after His baptism by John the Baptist and then by the Holy Spirit, was able to perform miracles of healing and perform miraculous demonstrations, which indicated that His words were backed by the authority of the one He claimed as was His Father. John 5:1–5 and 19–23. As in the healing of the man lowered through the roof of a house where Jesus was teaching. Mark 2:1–12. Even the dead were brought to life, as in the raising of Lazarus, John 11:28. Whilst in words He told of the love of God for humanity. But the coming of Jesus was not to happen until created mankind was ready to accept it. And the return of Christ to this earth will not occur until the time is ready for judgement.

No one has ever seen God, although His voice has been heard, simply because He does not exist in the sense of being composed of matter. However, in order that humanity might understand His attributes and His purpose for creation, we know that He sent His son, Jesus the Christ, who took on the human form in order to communicate directly with and engage personally with humanity. Which gives rise to the idea that the appearances of God in the Old Testament might actually refer to the presence of Jesus, referred to as 'the Lord'. Then, when the Jesus we see in the New Testament, having come to earth to live as a human with all its limitations and not as a spiritual being, had completed His work on earth and had returned to that spiritual world from which He came, God the Father sent His Holy Spirit. Who came to His disciples on the Day of Pentecost and remains here to be with all those who recognize and believe in His Son. Enabling them to experience the presence of God in their lives. This is why God is understood by Christians to have three different aspects. The origin of all things is pure Spirit. The God who related to humanity at the beginning in the Garden of Eden and will finally return to create a 'new heaven and a new earth' is referred to as God the Son because He was born to a human mother to become like one of us. Finally, when, after His death and resurrection, Jesus was seen to return to heaven from which He came, God, in mercy and love, made it possible for humankind to receive an eternal, everlasting spiritual presence in the person of the Holy Spirit, who came to the first disciples and apostles on the Day of Pentecost. The 'Adam' denied access to the 'Tree of Life' by his disobedience, Genesis 3:22, will finally be given access to the 'Tree of Life, Revelation 2:7'.

The most important thing we learn from this is that it is God the Father whom we worship. Yes, we are immeasurably grateful to Jesus for coming to earth, suffering, and dying in order to enable us to know God, but we must not forget that it is God the Father who loved the world so much that He gave us His son

(John 3:16). Many will understand what it means to lose a child, but God freely 'gave' us His Son because of His love. Jesus said, "He that hath seen Me hath seen the Father," but He also said, "I am going to the Father, for He is greater than I." And in John 14:28. Jesus also said, "Henceforth you will ask the Father in My name, and He will give you what you ask." John 15:16, if it is right for you to have it. Jesus also taught His disciples when they pray to say, "Our Father, which art in Heaven, hallowed be Thy name." Luke 11:2. Paul, the great apostle of the faith, said, speaking of the role of Jesus, "There is but one mediator between God and Man, Jesus Christ." 1 Timothy 2:5

Therefore, whilst we worship God the father, to approach Him our only access is through Jesus. No saints, however virtuous their lives, can intercede with God. Because they are dead, yes, but also because Jesus is clearly stated to be the ONLY mediator between us, the created beings, and God. This is where so much confusion has arisen in Christian belief, through introducing concepts and ideas which are not in the Bible. But the Bible is the only evidence for our Christian faith and contains all that we need to know. Man-made ideas are not relevant. The original Nicene Creed, which was agreed upon in that great conclave of the Church in Nicaea in 314 AD, settled once and for ever the basis of our Christian Faith, and that has not changed.

It is for this reason that we need to be extremely careful to avoid the many theories, reports of manifestations, and most especially those physical objects, which are claimed to represent God. The very first commandment was, "Thou shalt have no other gods," and then, "Thou shalt make to thyself no graven images." Exodus 20. Many very interesting books have been written about searching for 'The Holy Grail', supposedly a cup or vessel which is said to have been either the vessel from which our Lord drank at the 'Last Supper' or to have contained some of His blood from the Cross. We know from scripture that the Last Supper was prepared and eaten in a private house in Jerusalem as a family meal, Matthew 26:17–25, as was the regular practice at that time. Consequently, the vessels used would have been ordinary domestic household articles. To suggest that Jesus had or used any precious or valuable item is contrary to the whole manner of His life. Which was based on simplicity and the avoidance of external physical valuables. Possibly the only item of value which He possessed was the seamless robe He wore, which was probably provided by one of the wealthy women who supported Him and for which the soldiers at the crucifixion cast lots to gamble for it in one piece rather than destroy its value by cutting it in pieces.

In the case of a vessel supposedly containing the blood of Christ from the Cross, there was very little blood shed on the Cross. His head would have bled slightly when the soldiers put a rough crown of thorns on him, in mockery, and His back would possibly have bled slightly from the beating He was given, but neither was sufficient to provide a quantity which could be collected, and the soldiers would certainly not have bothered to collect any of it. When He hung on the Cross, the only reference to blood was when a soldier pierced His side, but again the quantity would have been slight. It was not the Roman custom to reduce the length of suffering by blood loss, and we know that although by evening Jesus was dead. In fact, Pilate was surprised to hear that Jesus was already dead when Nicodemus went to request Jesus' body and the other two criminals who were still alive were dispatched by breaking their legs. This was not an act of mercy, but because the Jews did not want bodies hanging on a cross after 6.00 pm because that was the start of the holy day, the Sabbath. A Jewish day was from 6.00 pm in the evening of each day, originating from Genesis 1:3, "And the evening and the morning were the first day."

It is the same principle with so-called 'relics', whether they be part of the original Cross or even bones. On a visit to the Top Kapi museum in Istanbul many years ago, I was shown what was called the 'thumb of John the Baptist'. The danger is that if we venerate objects like these, irrespective of the validity of the item, then the 'worship' or 'veneration' is focused on the object, not on God or Jesus.

Unlike most other religions, we are commanded that there are to be no physical, man-made images to represent the Christian God because He has no tangible form; He is pure spirit. Therefore, attempting to reproduce God in any physical form is impossible. Any image would be a travesty, a diminution of the majesty of our God, because it is not possible to represent Him physically.

Jesus, on the other hand, was God revealed in human form to make this invisible God known to us, and for this reason, and because of His suffering and sacrificial death in our place, we worship Him. The disciples twice heard a voice saying of Jesus, "This is My beloved Son in whom I am well pleased." The first occasion being at Jesus' baptism by his cousin John in the river Jordan, and the second on the Mount of Transfiguration, when the transfigured Jesus appeared, talking with Moses and Elijah in the presence of Peter, James, and John, and a voice came from the heavens, "This is my beloved Son; listen to Him."

One of the remarkable things about the visit to earth of the Son of God was that, amongst many other things, He came to make known to His 'disciples' and, through them, to the world, the whole point and purpose of this creation. Why it was created by God in the first place. And, even more remarkable, that we, that is, those who through their belief in God are marked out as 'chosen', would become His sons and daughters and share with Jesus the benefits and blessings of His inheritance, the perfect and holy 'new creation', which would replace this corrupted existence. 1 Peter 1:3–6.

These 'children of God', as they are called in the pages of the Bible, are described as being "chosen before the foundation of the world." Ephesians 1:4, and this theme is repeated by other writers such as Peter in his first epistle, who also refers to Christ as having been chosen "before the foundation of the world." 1 Peter 1:20.

This concept of a race of people chosen with a specific purpose warrants further exploration. It begins in then Old Testament with the singling out of one particular person, such as Abraham, to become the progenitor, first of the 'chosen race', the Jewish nation, and then, after the nation had rejected his descendant, Jesus of Nazareth, the Son of God, before Pontius Pilate, the Roman governor, the promise was opened out to all people, irrespective of nationality, creed, or colour. So Abraham then becomes a symbol of things in the future.

Right at the start, when God singled out Abraham with the promise of a nation and a country for him and his descendants, God had already projected that through Abraham all families of the earth shall be blessed. Genesis 12:3. Here again is a foretelling, long before the idea was recognised, of what Jesus, who was both a direct descendant of Abraham and also the Son of God, would accomplish through His life and death. Which occurred after the 'children of Abraham', the Jews, had rejected him, saying, Matthew 27:25, "Not this man but Barabbas," and John 18:37–40. "We will not have this man rule over us."

This incident is part of the evidence that, behind the whole of scripture, we can find a symbolic theme, which creates a continual reference to things in the future. It is vital, therefore, that we examine both the source of this information and the reasoning behind it. Most particularly because this information is also linked to the concept that this world, this universe as we currently perceive it, is not only evolving as a continuing process but destined to be destroyed, either in part, such as this planet on which we live, or the whole universe. And the purpose being for it to be replaced with something which is more permanent. Romans 8:20. And the reason for this is stated to be that this planet and its inhabitants are flawed. Corrupt and self-destructive. The story of Adam and Eve describes the development of moral consciousness and the problems which it brought (Genesis 3:22). Leading also to the concept that this 'creation as we know it is a proving ground, a period of testing and elimination, preparatory to the establishing of a more perfect world. The idea of which is developed through the teaching of the New Testament'.

This idea or concept is revolutionary because it implies that there is a moral authority or force which is and has been active in the creationary process, whether that was a single event or a very lengthy process. A concept which is quite contrary to the idea that the formation of the vast universe is simply the result of a natural process, whether that be the 'big bang' or some other initial cause. What science does not answer is simply where the material, particles or elements from which the particles evolved came from in the first place or what set it in motion.

One of the earliest and most clear illustrations of this concept of a purposeful creation is to be found in the life of the man seen by Jews, Christians, and Muslims as the founder of their 'faith'. Namely Abraham, who was called by 'God' to leave his established position in the city or region of Ur in the Chaldees to go out Westward to seek a 'city which hath foundations, whose builder and maker is God'. Hebrews 11:10. This concept would lead, as we have seen, to the establishing of, amongst others, the Jewish nation with its homeland in that territory, which was known as Palestine and is now defined as the area known as Israel. This was intended to be a nation, distinguished from its neighbours by being ruled by God and to be living in accordance with a set of laws known basically as the Ten Commandments and later defined in greater detail known as the Torah. Which were being administered, first by single figures, known as the Patriarchs, then by appointed Judges, and ultimately by persons known as Kings, who were guided by prophets and priests, men chosen by God who were given authority and expertise directly by Him, being able to communicate with Him. However, the promise of the land of Canaan, which was originally given to Abraham (Genesis 12) when God told him to leave the city of Ur in Mesopotamia, was a conditional one. And, whilst the sons of Abraham, Isaac and Jacob, were largely true to that covenant, their descendants became increasingly unwilling to keep their side of the agreement. They wanted the benefits of God's blessing and the security of His help, but their responsibilities, their observance of their obligation towards God, became increasingly disregarded. We might well question whether they deserve to have remained a unique nation. Abraham lived there for some time but left with his immediate family at a time of great famine. Under God's guidance, one of Abraham's sons, Joseph, was used by God to become the deliverer of his family and enable its development into a nation. Because under the blessing of God the one who had been rejected by his brothers had, under God's unique blessing, become the governor of the whole nation under the King. Once again, a projection of the role of Jesus, who was also rejected by His 'family' but is now, and will soon be seen to be, the King of all existence, The Kingdom of God.

The Israelite nation flourished and ultimately was seen as a threat to the security of the Egyptian nation, resulting, some years later, in their status being reduced from that of shepherds and herdsmen to utter slavery, as they were made to construct new cities in the area known as Goshen. God then used another of Abraham's descendants, Moses, to deliver them and lead them back into their own country, Canaan. Once again, they failed to live up to the terms of the Covenant by compromising with the existing inhabitants and became a nation of separate tribes. Under David the nation was united at last, and his son, Solomon, built on his father's legacy to make the united nation one of the most prosperous and militarily strong forces in that whole area, with the glorious Temple, which he built as the focus of their worship. That unity lasted for around 100 years, from 1030–931 BC. Then, after Solomon's death, they became divided into two separate nations for about a further 170 years. In the South, Judah, who also had the Temple in Jerusalem as their religious focal point, lived under kings who, in the majority, were loyal to their covenanted heritage and supported the Temple. Whilst in the North, which kept the name Israel with its capital, Samaria, built their own separate altars for worship. The South remained more loyal to their heritage, whilst the North lost sight of their responsibilities to their God and were finally overrun by the Assyrians in 722, despite the challenges of some very outspoken prophets like Elijah and Elisha, who repeatedly warned the nation of impending disaster.

The South managed to retain its integrity for some 100 years, but finally they too were conquered by the Babylonians in 586 BC, who, because of their rebellious nature, finally destroyed the city and the Temple and exiled all the inhabitants.

The exile of the Jews lasted for some 70 years, until the Persian king Cyrus, who had replaced the Assyrians and the Babylonians as the dominant power in that area, allowed them to return and the foundations of the Temple were laid. But despite the admonitions of prophets like Ezra and Nehemiah, progress in reconstruction was slow, and the exiles also were slow in returning to the Southern kingdom. In the North, the population never formally returned, and the inhabitants who had remained or who did return were, at the time of Jesus, known as 'Samaritans' and were despised by the true traditional Jews in Judah. (See John 4:3–30 for our Lord's encounter with the woman of Samaria.). However, as is so often the case, our Lord's story of the help given to an injured Jewish man by a Samaritan, Luke 10:30–37, shows that one must not condemn a whole race because of past failures, and here, in this story, the actions of the Samaritan are used as an example of true charity, as opposed to the Priest and Levite who used their religious convictions to avoid helping.

The Persians who authorized the return of the Southern Jews were replaced in turn by the Greeks under Alexander the Great and then by the Romans as the controlling power in Western Mesopotamia. There were two important issues during this period. First, that Judea was seen as important by the various rising empires because it sat astride the Way of the Sea, which was the major coastal route to Egypt, which was the other major empire to the southwest, and therefore needed to be under the control of the advancing forces. The second was that whilst the conquering powers tended to encourage the dominant local religious groups in the hope that, by encouraging and supporting them, they would gain the cooperation of the native peoples. Israel during those years was also suffering from internal conflict. From the dominant and rebellious Maccabean tribes and the conflict between the two religious groups, the Pharisees, who favoured the authority of the royal leaders, and the more aristocratic Sadducees, who wanted more religious power.

The Persians were finally routed, in 313 BC, by the Greeks under Alexander the Great. On his death aged just 33, power fell into the hands of his generals, and Judea became part of the conflict which arose between the Greeks, who had occupied Northern Egypt, and the encroaching Romans, who were now replacing them as the dominant power in West Euphrates.

Jerusalem finally fell to the Romans under Herod in 38/7 B.C., and it was he who, to encourage the loyalty of the Jews, built or rebuilt the Temple, which was such a source of wonder to Jesus' disciples. But such was the turbulent nature of the time that the Romans built a fort within the walls of the city and maintained a number of soldiers there under the authority of the Roman governor Pontius Pilate. And so this was the situation when our Lord began His ministry. The Pharisees and the Sadducees had authority over the nation's religious affairs, but political power rested with the occupying Romans. Hence, they alone had the power to impose the death penalty.

Israel had first achieved greatness under the leadership of King David, who was known for two things. His great courage and ability as a military leader, beginning with his slaying of the giant Goliath and then his success in battle as a soldier, won him the respect of the people and, sadly, the jealousy of King Saul. But possibly his greatest success came from his love for God, exhibited so continually during his life and through the many psalms or songs of praise to God which he composed. His reign was noted for his reliance on God through the priests. Men like Samuel. David reigned for forty years altogether. Seven as King of Judah and thirty-three as king of the united nation.

Solomon was able to build on this, but his wealth was probably drawn mostly from taxes and trade from the ancient trade route which followed the coast and was known as the Way of the Sea. His wisdom was a gift of God, but sadly, in later life he turned more and more away from the worship of God. Basically because of his multiple wives, whom he married for political reasons but whom he allowed to follow the worship of their own native heather gods, even to building temples for them adjacent to God's own Temple, which he had built following his father's instructions.

Today we still have issues over the connection between state and church, as we shall consider later. For example, is our present King divinely appointed to rule, or is he merely there by ancestral heritage? Is he the head of the Church in England, or is his role purely political? Yet historically the power of the monarch is restricted by Parliament.

Chapter 2
The Source of Our Information

The earliest source of our information concerning God and His relationship with His creation came from what we know as The Bible. Until some 150 years ago, the Old Testament was seen as a Jewish religious textbook, designed to justify both Jewish history and the formation of what became a unique faith, Judaism, and then leading out of it in the New Testament, we have the transition to a universal religious faith, open to the whole human race irrespective of nationality, which we call the Christian Church. It was not seen as a scientific or even an historical record but something which a reader would accept by 'faith' as being relevant.

However, almost out of the blue, as it were, in the early part of the nineteenth century, something happened which would radically and dramatically change the worldview of the Bible. The reason the Old Testament record could now be verified as factually accurate by archaeological discovery, for archaeological exploration was uncovering names and places which previously were simply names in a book. Now there was evidence of their existence. The book "The Bible as History" by Werner Keller, published in the early 1960s, lists and illustrates how much of this modern archaeology has shown that the places and events of the Bible can be corroborated, and since then the latest excavations in Palestine and the Middle East have revealed even more evidence, as have the excavations in Egypt.

Yes, the Bible is a collection of accounts, which probably date from around 1,500 B.C., the earliest manuscripts being in Hebrew, the Jewish language, or Aramaic, the language of the area known as West Euphrates, and which were collated and incorporated in the Greek language after the conquest by Alexander the Great, bringing their learning to vast areas of central Europe and the adjacent

Asian countries, such as Turkey. But the Bible also covers a period of a further 2,000 years earlier, a time before mankind had evolved a method of recording events. The earliest known approximations to what we know as writing have been found to come from two sources: the Sumeric cuneiform script and the pictographic detail of the Egyptians, as seen in their temples However, three things need to be borne in mind. First, that there was a great burst of knowledge about four thousand years ago, the time when in England the people of that area round Salisbury Plain were building their great Temple to the sun known to us as Stonehenge. This was also true of the great area known as the Fertile Crescent, in what we now know as Mesopotamia, which stretched from the Nile valley in Egypt, North Africa, westwards to cover the great rivers of Tigris and Euphrates, the Persian Gulf, and the area to the east of that. This was the time of the building of the Pyramids in Egypt and the rise of kings and gods in Mesopotamia, whilst new discoveries in the twentieth century would also find even earlier habitations and temple cults in places like Malta and Gozo, which still puzzle science because they suggest learning, knowledge, and understanding of the universe which are inexplicable.

The second thing to consider is that for many years the only knowledge of this area, known to us now as 'the fertile crescent', had its source in the Old Testament of the Bible. But, equally, this was not regarded as being historically accurate until the early part of the nineteenth century, when, for some reason, historians decided to explore those areas archaeologically and, to their surprise, found in ancient Sumerian and Egyptian writings not only records but also, as they dug, they found actual artifacts with depictions of kings and rulers, of gods and of cities, and evidence of civilisations of that earlier period. Here, suddenly, was the record in actual fact of those years in that area; details of names and places in the Bible now emerged, facts about those historic years that not even the Greeks and Romans had been aware of. Now at last there was hard evidence of the historical facts. Suddenly the scholastic world woke to the fact that the evidence was there, to be excavated and explored. Names found in the Bible became places. Dr Werner Keller's masterpiece, 'The Bible as History', first published in Germany in 1955 and translated into English in the following years, covers this explosion of knowledge in scholastic detail, as I first became aware when I obtained a copy. This masterpiece explores in detail the discoveries which were made in the early 19th century and which are still being made of the early Biblical period before written records were available.

The third point to note is that until these early nineteenth-century discoveries, most people regarded the Old Testament as being largely symbolic but did not believe it to be based on factually accurate records. That its cities and rulers were actual people and places. Now, with the discovery of artifacts and scrolls bearing the same details that were found in the Old Testament, it was understood at last that these places and events existed and occurred.

Yes, the first part of the Old Testament, from the Creation up to the time of Abraham, was based on verbal memories passed down and, probably written by the priests of the Jewish faith, it would have included Jewish versions of the mythological tales of pre-history, which we now know were current. The Jewish versions of these 'events' were designed to explain the origins of their unique Jewish faith. That may well account for the fact that both Christianity and Islam date the beginning of their faith to the life of Abraham. Matthew, in his gospel, when listing the ancestors of Jesus, does not go back further than Abraham because it was to him and his descendants that God made the original promises and to whom He gave the contractual sign of circumcision. The Old Testament traces Abraham's descent from Seth, one of Noah's three sons who survived the great flood by miraculous intervention. Which was to them the construction of the Ark. The Bible does not include scientific evidence of creation because, even when it was written down, knowledge, which included mathematical truths and an awareness of the sky above with its regular appearance of the sun, the moon, and the planets, could not conceive the vastness of what we now take as commonplace. But evidence is now there to be seen of events like the great flood, the existence of buildings like the Tower of Babel, and the slavery of people under Egyptian rule. Just as later documents, record the capture of the Northern kingdom of Israel by the Assyrians and the later capture of the Southern kingdom of Judah by the Chaldeans and their destruction of its temple in 586 BC.

In the same way, stories of a great flood were told by people of many nations. The Greeks also had their version, and many other nations have versions which are still recounted today. However, the greatest evidence was found by archaeologists who were excavating at the ancient city of Ur, who found below the levels of more recent dwellings evidence of a much earlier period but covered in clay containing myriads of marine creatures. Therefore, whilst the early Old Testament may not be an historically accurate account, many of its events were based on verbal records passed down of early events, which recent archaeological evidence confirms as having occurred at some time in the past.

However, symbolically the story of eight 'good' people being saved from annihilation by being caught up in a boat would become symbolic of a select people being saved from disaster by God's intervention. As would happen repeatedly to the Jewish people, and could be symbolic of God's love and mercy offering hope and deliverance to those who put their trust in him. The account of how one man and his sons constructed a huge vessel on dry land, nowhere near water, is an illustration again of what the Bible calls 'faith', belief in a supernatural event.

The Bible is probably the world's greatest piece of literature, covering as it does a period of some 4,000 years, describing the origins and the development of a nation of people whose presence on the world stage would change the course of history. In recording the crucial years of its history, it describes the lives and characters of a unique race of people, tracing their historical and geographical development and later their political development from single individuals to their emergence as one of the great nations of their day, a nation which today is still at the centre of world history. Modern historical research in looking back relies largely upon archaeological exploration and the discovery of artifacts to determine events. The Bible, by contrast, deals with the personal lives of these people by recording their actions in response to the events which shaped their lives and those of their descendants. The narrative also traces the developing physical, psychological, and mental awareness of these members of humanity as they come to terms with incredible problems and difficulties. But, most remarkably and in a manner not seen anywhere else in any written form, it also foretells, or predicts, major events before they happen. Usually either giving a reason for the predicted events or telling of a way to escape the consequences. As happened with the account of Noah and the great flood, in which he was not only warned of an impending disastrous flood but also told to construct a life-saving boat for himself and his family. But, even more remarkably, he was given details of how to construct it, on dry land, before the disastrous flood occurred. This evidence of pre-warning of events which would later occur is characteristic of the Old Testament. What makes the Bible so crucially, so vitally important for us and our society today is that the Bible makes clear the principle that Creation was the considered plan of a totally omnipotent being, wholly outside of time and human knowledge. A Creator who, through the presence on earth of His Son, whom He made visible in a form which made Him able to be understood by humanity. created all things which are in existence and then sent this son into that world to maintain its existence, deal with its anticipated failures, and then 'recreate' humanity and ultimately recreate the whole of the universe. In this Book He has warned of an even greater disaster to come, which will involve the whole universe. However, even though people at large do not attach much importance to this source, science is now adding its voice to an alarming extent in warning of an imminent impending disaster for a universe which is progressively being degraded by human demands. Namely, the acquisitive requirements of what we call 'industrialisation'.

However, the Bible alerts us now to the fact that previous warnings to the Jewish nation, which went unheeded, as recoded in their own Book of Laws, which we refer to as the Old Testament, resulted in disaster for that first 'chosen' race, the Jewish nation. The original promise made to Abraham, of a land and a civilization which would be a blessing and an example to the rest of the world, was lost because they, as a nation, failed to keep to the terms of the contract, which were obedience to the Laws (Exodus 20) and reverence for their God, which would be demonstrated by honesty and compassion in their relationship with each other. So that whilst the first commandment was to love God, the second was to love their neighbour.

After a long period of growth in number, most notably during their period in Egypt, which itself was brought about by seven years of famine, their number grew from about 70 persons (Genesis 46:27) who went into Egypt as guests of Joseph and the Pharaoh, who appointed him as governor because of his prescience in predicting and preparing for the seven-year famine. to number some 2,000,000 when they left many years later, after a period of some 400 years in Egypt. We are not told the exact number of persons who left Egypt, but we are told that they had 603,550 men aged 20–50 years who were fit for service as soldiers. Numbers 1:46. However, allowing for all those younger and older men and the women, the total number was probably more than 2 million persons.

What we may not recognise is that the Bible also discusses the prospect of saving this planet from destruction. An event which is inevitable unless we change our understanding of what is happening and do something about it. This is where a study of history with the events which happened, the people, and their response, or lack of it, can be vital for us. Because we are now facing unprecedented changes in things like our climate, social interaction, and international conflict on an unprecedented scale. Politically, economically, socially, and geologically, we are entering a period of uncertainty and unpredictable change. These are matters which may appear to be out of our control but which, nevertheless, threaten the future of life on earth as we know it. But the Bible contains the answer for those who are willing to read it and understand it. Which is a belief in and obedience to God.

Even more remarkable is the fact that the Bible also records the development of a nation within a nation, the emergence of a great number of unique characters exhibiting almost supernatural skills as they come forward at critical moments in the nation's history to deliver and rescue the nation by heroic and selfless acts. Acts which indicate a belief or trust in something greater than themselves, a hope for which they were prepared to accept the enormous price of self-sacrifice. A record which suggests that there is both a plan and a guiding force behind or underlying what we perceive as history, which suggests that there is a purpose for all this. That there is a future which has been and still is being revealed to those who know where to look for it. Yet this source is one which is most frequently misunderstood or simply ignored, but believe me, it will engulf the whole of the existing universe, with horrifying consequences for those who disregard the warnings. This narrative is at best an attempt to open people's eyes to the inherent self-destructive nature of human existence as we know it. To warn us of the fact that we are headed at increasing velocity towards oblivion and to demonstrate that it is not too late to save this planet but that this requires immediate and very challenging changes.

An incident in the Old Testament which illustrates this is found in the history of the founding father of the Jewish nation, Abraham. Who, as we have seen, was told to leave the well-established community of the city of Ur in the Chaldees, leaving behind the established comfort and security of a well-organized social community, to look for 'a city which hath foundations, whose builder and maker is God'. Hebrews 11:8–11. In other words, to trust in the guidance of an authority which was outside of human knowledge or understanding. What we would call 'faith'. But it is also indicative of the fact that Christians also see this life as something which will be replaced by something far better in the future.

The narrative of the Old Testament is dominated by men and some women who are marked out as specially endowed with abilities beyond normal, people who, later in the New Testament, will be described as 'chosen'. And it is by observing these marked people and comparing them with their neighbours that we are able to see the beginning of a master plan, not for this creation but for a new creation which will ultimately replace it. And in this sense they too become symbolic figures. Representative in their age but having a reference to future events.

It is this 'master plan' for the universe which was made known to a chosen few through the life on earth of the 'the Son of God', who called Himself "the son of man." Who was born supernaturally into human flesh and whose human life was seen as a mirror of the ideal person. One who was approved of by God. In fact, at His baptism in the river Jordan by John the Baptist, a voice was heard which said, "This is my beloved son, in whom I am well pleased." Luke 3:22 And again on that spectacular vision on the Mount of Transfiguration, the same voice said, "This is my beloved son, whom I have chosen; listen to Him." Luke 9:35. So Jesus also becomes an example of the ideal servant of God.

Contrary to the view that God is simply a loving and generous influence, we are increasingly made aware through the narrative that God is actively involved with humanity and that He is influencing the lives of those who respond to Him. So, a vital component of the God/Human relationship is defined by the fact that He knows and can control the future. Which also means that He deals with individuals according to His pre-knowledge of how that individual will respond. God is never taken by surprise. Effectively, God exists outside of time in the geophysical sense. Our times and seasons, our days and our years, are determined by the earth's rotation round the sun. God is eternally existent. For Him there is no yesterday or today; life is just one timeless panorama. For us, life is an ongoing process which ultimately ages and decays, but God is 'ever present'. For Him there is no past, present, or future; the whole scene exists like a completed drawing or design. Just as the finished house is depicted by the architect before work commences, the building work must then comply with the scheme agreed by the planning authority. We need to accept that God is beyond our understanding; all we can do is seek His guidance and surrender ourselves to His will for us.

I once stood on top of a hill in Wales and watched the progress of a train as it followed the line around the hill. Passengers could, at any given moment, remember from whence they had come and could see where they were, but they could not 'know' what lay ahead. Neither would they be aware of the whole complexity of the national and international rail network of which theirs was just a minute part. God is the architect of creation, and He has designed it for a purpose, in which He has chosen that humanity will play a part. Unlike an

44

architect who may meet unexpected problems, God is aware of every part of the future. Consequently, His knowledge and response mean that every contingency has already been dealt with.

There is clear evidence for this statement in the Bible. The most straightforward is found in the writings of that Master theologian of the early Church, St Paul. In his letter to the Ephesian Church in chapter 1:14, he says, "Even before the world was made, God had already chosen us to be His through our union with Christ." This concept is also implied in his letter to Hebrews 2:5–8; Peter also picks up this idea in his first letter 1:1–2. And there are many other references to the same principle, just as Paul says of himself in his letter to the Romans 1:1 when he calls himself an 'apostle chosen and called by God'. This idea of the whole of the existing creation being part of a greater plan is also made clear by Paul in his letter to Romans 8:19. "All of creation waits with eager longing for God to reveal His children. For creation was condemned to lose its purpose, not of its own will but because God willed it to be so. Yes, there was the hope that creation itself would one day be set free from its slavery to decay and would share the glorious freedom of the children of God."

It is worth mentioning at this point that the previous quotation, that 'creation itself was condemned to lose its purpose – because God willed it to be so', could well be the reason why we are seeing so many violent and unparalleled changes in climate, as well as the political and social unrest and militant activity, and an increase in outbreaks of disease, plagues, and utter poverty. Because all of this was predicted by Jesus, Matthew chapter 24. Which means that it is a sign of His imminent return to sort things out. Imminent in the sense that the universe is billions of years old, whereas the Bible only covers a period of some 6,000 years, of which some 2,000 years have passed since Jesus said it.

The Bible is, by any standards, a remarkable book, which is still selling in massive quantities all over the world. One of the reasons for its popularity is that right from the earliest pages it predicts future events, things which could not possibly have been known at the time. A time which begins before writing, as we know, it had been invented. These events could not have been known or foreseen. Let alone understood, even at the later time when events were being recorded in writing. Even now, at this moment as you are now reading these words, the world is in turmoil. Inexplicable weather, the cause of which science attempts to explain; universal worldwide plagues and unremitting war and conflict, creating massive casualties amongst the civilian population;

earthquakes and other physical afflictions. And nowhere is there a political or scientific answer. Those who read the Bible can see that events like these were foretold in the pages of scripture, but even more alarming is that the Bible predicts even more disturbing events which are yet to happen. The Bible provides a record of past events so that we can see the errors in individuals and society which caused these problems. It becomes a startling record of actions and the reactions in order that future generations might be able to avoid making the same mistakes. Henry Ford, the founder of the vast Ford Motor industry, is quoted as saying that 'all history is bunk', but presumably that was because, in his view, what was hindering social and economic progress was our reluctance to accept change. His introduction of different methods of manufacturing, such as conveyor belt construction for motor cars, enabled him to increase productivity and at the same time reduce production costs, bringing the motor car to the masses.

However, equally valid is the comment that if we ignore history, we fail to learn from the mistakes of the past and simply repeat them. Therefore, by not looking back, we fail to benefit from experience. The Bible, with its record of human activity, limited though it may be in some respects, can be seen as a history of mankind, and, because it relates to man's relationship with the God who is its creator, it reflects the place of mortal humanity in the created universe. By recording the mistakes made by our ancestors and the tragic outcome, we are given the opportunity to remedy the situation. However, we are also shown just how powerless mankind is in so many respects and just how powerful the active force behind nature really is. Evidenced in the recent violent storms, the repeated earthquakes, and the volcanic activity. And these, as geological and archaeological evidence reveal, were far more violent and active in the past, responsible for creating this planet as we know it today. So that we become actors on the stage of an ongoing drama. In danger of ignoring the script because we think that we know better what to do. The basic flaw in all this is human nature, which, at its best, is determined and driven by self-interest, but so powerless when faced with a constantly active nature. We are genetically driven by the most dominant human factors of self-preservation and the search for knowledge. However, one thing separates man from achieving his goal, and that is the basic human self-destructive flaw, the basic weakness of all flesh, which is the desire to pursue those natural desires which are destructive. As opposed to this we have the creator's offer of a solution, not derived via the flawed human nature but by a supernatural event, namely the coming of Christ, the Son of God, into human nature to demonstrate the only solution to innate corruption, by one through whose death we are offered deliverance from evil and by whose subsequent resurrection we are given the potential of hope for an eternal future, perfect and free from all ills, which we will share with the Son of God Himself.

Essentially then, the Biblical account is designed to deal with human conduct, its beliefs and behaviour, in order to demonstrate the flaws inherent in human nature and the only way to overcome this. Its main purpose is not as an account of physical or geological history; it is an account of human activity and the way in which humanity came to terms with forces which were beyond their understanding. The Old Testament is descriptive of one race and their conflict with their own related peoples and illustrates the underlying cause of their ultimate failure and downfall. A narrative which, following the initial failure of this unique nation, then reaches out to the whole of humanity in the New Testament, offering a new hope, a new way of life, and the potential of a glorious future. A hope which is even more relevant for us today as we face the total failure of modern society to purge itself, to renew its physical and social standards, to prevent the breakdown of personal and international relationships, let alone find an answer to a deteriorating physical environment. Without God, the whole universe is doomed to extinction.

We now accept that the earliest parts of the Bible were largely based on oral evidence, prehistory, because it refers to a time before alphabetic writing had been discovered. But what was known was treasured and passed down to succeeding generations, because it defined their unique identity. This was particularly true of family relationships, were treasured because they provided the evidence of their claim to God's promises. Unfortunately, for many people, the early chapters of the Bible can be a problem because they recount events which we may not be able to place archaeologically or date accurately, although modern archaeological discoveries have provided a great deal of hitherto hidden evidence. But in many cases they contain important ideas which are of importance and relevant to our modern world. To understand these early events, such as the account of creation, we need to recognise the authors' ignorance of even the basic facts of the universe as we now know it. Although we now recognise that knowledge existing at the time showed great skill and ability in calculating, for example, the movements of the planets and the brighter stars and in the construction of their great monuments. But even the concept of the earth rotating around the sun rather than placing the earth as the centre of the universe was rejected by the Church of the day, which wanted to believe that spiritually the planet earth was the centre of God's universe. Men like Galileo were outlawed by the Church of their day, which refused to accept anything which refuted their 'religious' ideas, which sadly were wrong, and this may have undermined an acceptance of what is Biblical fact.

An example of this is to be found in the account of Adam and Eve. Most scholars accept that it is 'pre-history' because there are no supporting means of identifying such a period of time, either in archaeology or geology. Some suggest that the story was 'created' much later by religious scholars attempting to explain the origins of humanity and the presence of God as the great creator to counter other, mythological explanations which were extant at the time and that for this purpose they used contemporary existing myths as a basis. That may be the case, but what marks the Genesis story out for us is that symbolically it contains information about events which would not happen for some 4,000 years. Namely that Eve's seed, a child born to a woman, would destroy the evil or self-destructive element in human nature. "Her offspring will crush your head, and you will bite her offspring's heel." (Genesis 3:15.) Which instantly implies information which it was impossible for the human mind to know. It also answers the question of how 'sin' entered the world. The couple had been guilty of disobedience in order to achieve knowledge. The discovery was that with knowledge comes the potential of 'sin'. Their error was that they were disobedient to a command or law. This was not a chance act; it was a deliberate choice, and the punishment for their disobedience was defined physically as pain in childbirth for the woman and hard work for the man, but in religious terms the punishment was to be death. Spiritual death in the break of their daily fellowship with God and later physical death. 'Evil' here is being personified in the form of a snake, a creature whose bite could be fatal. This concept of actions having other than physical consequences suggests a 'divine', or other than human, intervention and retribution, and this personification of good and evil provides a theme which is continued throughout the book.

What is interesting is that, as we have seen, recent archaeological discoveries provide evidence which support many of these Biblical events. For example, there is evidence of a massive flood in the area of the Eastern Mediterranean which caused salt water to enter the existing fresh waters of what is now the Black Sea, where there is evidence of the remains of freshwater fish, and other writings contain evidence of people escaping a vast flood by building a boat. The Biblical record may simply have been one way of coming to terms with things which were beyond a primitive mind to comprehend but seeing it as a valuable way to instruct and to teach future generations. What we do know is that several similar accounts appear in the earliest written records, in Babylonian and Chaldean mythology. Where the Bible account differs is that whereas the other accounts refer to a multiplicity of gods, the Biblical account refers only to one supreme being. Therefore, when the earliest scribes began to record their own history, they used it to promote the ideas which were current at their time of writing to illustrate their views of the omnipotence of their God. Therefore, the Jewish God, Yahweh or Jehovah, is seen as the creator, and in that sense, Adam and Eve can be seen as metaphoric or symbolic accounts of the origin of 'sin' and the conflict between good and evil. Remember that it was well into the 'Middle Ages' before the principle of the earth going round the sun was established. Anything which could not be understood was attributed to supernatural forces. Further, as there was no written language at the time, the early parts of the Bible would have been constructed later from memories passed down. What we do know is that the major issue raised by the Bible is that God is declared to be the Creator of the Universe. How and why are not revealed because they were not understood. What did matter was that these people who would come to be called Israel and later referred to simply as Jews were a unique race because they believed in only one God. All the other nations had a multiplicity of gods, usually seen as the source of things which they could not understand. First gods of natural processes, such as the forces of nature, the elements, and the seasons, then later, gods of varying human attributes, such as love and war, as well as sickness and disease.

However, before long, as we read, we become aware first that these are not simply random events, because underlying everything is the sense, portrayed in action and in word, that there is an underlying plan, a purpose, and then we are made aware that there is a third person in the context, whose presence we become aware of gradually. We are three. The individual character involved, the reader who is there as an observer, but behind the scenes is another, whose nature, character, and personality will become evident through the pages of the book.

We may ask the question, 'Why does the Bible begin with just two people, Adam and Eve?' When we are told that after Cain killed Abel, Cain went out, married a wife, and founded a city (Genesis 4:17). Because this illustrates the fact that there must have been other people around at that time. So why begin the book of Genesis with Adam and Eve? One answer to that is that much later, when the first Jewish records were being expressed in writing, Adam and Eve may well have been seen by those later generations as the first identifiable ancestors of the race which would become 'the children of God'. If one looks at the first book of Chronicles, one can see how many descendants there were, but out of each family group, only one person, or one tribe, eventually emerge as the direct ancestors of the 'chosen race'. Many of the other branches of the family founded tribes and nations, some of which fought against this chosen race. As we shall later see. That may be why, from the depiction of Adam and Eve to the events such as the story of Noah and the Flood and the construction of the tower of Babylon, we have such a sketchy outline of the characters involved. It may be that they were seen and depicted as metaphorical or symbolic examples of 'sin', evil and the justice of God. In the same way that the characters of Adam and Eve were used to depict the introduction of morality and sin as being acts of disobedience to God, observed in their early ancestors. Actions against a supreme being who, as creator, had the right to demand both obedience and respect and who was seen as the ultimate arbiter of 'fate' or destiny. However, we must not dismiss these people and events as being purely mythological, because these events do have some basis in archaeological and geographical evidence. Increasing evidence of which is now emerging in the continuing recent discoveries, which actually began in the nineteenth century. For example, the geophysical evidence of a great flood in what is now Southern Turkey having occurred. An example of this is seen in the recently discovered evidence that what is now the Black Sea had once been fresh water. One solution put forward is that a sudden event, such as a tsunami, resulting from a known massive volcanic eruption. This enormous tsunami could well have raised the levels of the Mediterranean to the point when the whole of that area was inundated, causing a massive inflow of salt water. What later written records, including the decoding of an ancient cuneiform tablet found in Mesopotamia by Dr Finkel, have proved is that there were several records of massive floods. As in the Deucalion records, which put the date of one such flood as 1581 B.C. There are also similar reports of a massive flood found in the Torah, in the Quran, and also recorded by Josephus in his historical account of the Jewish nation, "The Antiquities." To the people of that time, a massive flood of that dramatic extent would, to the local people without any knowledge of anything outside their immediate neighbourhood, suggest to them that the area covered the whole of 'their world'. Which is the area in which they were living. The ancient records also tell of very detailed instructions on how to construct a large boat. Some years ago, a one-fifth-size replica was built, weighing some 37 tons, and it floated. The Jewish historians of that time would have been the priests, and they would have seen this event as being another example of their God punishing sin and saving a limited number of people. Those who were directly in the line of 'godly' persons. So that with Noah being a person whose godly ancestry was known, it would be an occasion when they could write out all the other people who were outside of God's purpose and focus on the descendants of Noah's three sons, Shem, Ham, and Japheth. So that the story of Noah having escaped a flood could well be historically accurate, even if the details had been exaggerated to increase the majesty of their God. In the same way, the description of the Tower of Babel fits the evidence of what were known as ziggurats ' large towers constructed in the same period of 'pre-history' and for which the accounts in scripture may be a potential source. In that sense, the Bible events were based on actual events but used by the priests to illustrate their thesis of the purity of their descendants, with the hand of God seen as the cause of these 'disasters'.

However, from the evidence given, it is quite clear that at the time of the Biblical account of Adam and Eve, 'civilisation' had reached a point which is now quite well understood in archaeological terms. For example, the people of 'The Garden of Eden' were cultivating the land. They were no longer simply hunter-gatherers. Civilisation had reached the point at which people were living in groups and required habitable settlements in order both to till the ground and secure those areas from attack. Adam and Eve were told to take control of their environment and care for it.

Further, they understood the concept of 'worship' and of the need to sacrifice to 'propitiate' their God. Adam and Eve's two children represented two aspects of farming typical of their period in history. Cain brought as a sacrifice the product of agrarian or arable farming, whilst Abel brought the product of pastoral farming. And it was Abel's offering, which involved the slaughter of an animal, which was approved. This action is exactly what would later underpin their relationship with God, pointing towards the concept of propitiation for 'sin'. However, for Cain to kill his brother out of jealousy, a passion which apparently arose because of a sacrifice to their god, implies that worship with its attendant need to propitiate or appease their god was an established fact even at this early stage in their development. Something which was recognized as being very important. Important enough to cause jealousy and violence, which is a characteristic of many similar situations in families, which can cause conflict. In other words, the incident can be seen both as an individual event and a warning of the potential dangers inherent in human society.

One conclusion which we can draw from this is that, central to the narrative of the Bible is a concern with one group of people, the ancestors of the Semitic race who, later, were descendants of Noah's son Shem, and it is these people who would, in due course, become the people of God, whom we know now as Jews. And it is these people on whose lives the Bible focuses, even though the narrative accepts that there were other races, other nationalities, and groupings which remain outside of this singular group. Therefore, whilst we confine our main study to the people, the races and tribes, which are the subject of the Bible, we cannot totally ignore the other peoples who may have lived at the time of the Biblical narrative, because they are also there in scripture for a purpose.

So, why read the Bible? The answer is two-fold. First, the way in which the characters are presented and the way in which they react to circumstances teaches us a lot about human behaviour but more important than this is the fact that a record of their behaviour, what we describe as the Word of God, is there and has been for thousands of years to teach us about God and about our relationship with Him. It teaches not only that God is in control of circumstances and situations but also that these people and events have much to teach us and all succeeding generations in demonstrating that this God loves and cares for us and that, through His Word, He is able to speak to us today. Much later, in the New Testament, it will be revealed that He is not some ethical concept but a living reality who, in the person of His Son Jesus Christ, was born into humanity through a young woman and the Holy Spirit and has lived amongst us and therefore fully understands the human condition.

Chapter 3
'Your Majesty, the Jews'

It is reported that King George IV once asked the then Astronomer Royal, Lord Herschel, "Prove to me that the Bible is true in one sentence." To which Lord Herschel replied, 'Your Majesty, the Jews'. The same idea is also attributed to King Frederick of Prussia, who reputedly asked his physician to explain miracles. To which the physician replied, "Your Majesty, the evidence is the continuing existence of the Jews." Whilst Louis XIV of France was also credited with a similar question when he asked the philosopher, Blaise Pascall, to justify the existence of miracles. To which Pascall replied, "Why the Jews, your majesty?"

The most remarkable thing about the Jewish nation is that it has outlasted all other nations and empires, and despite being homeless for the greater part of its time, it has retained its unique racial identity for some 4,000 years, dating its origins to the life of its founding father, Abraham, some 2,000 years BC. Remarkably, his descendants to this day still retain the unique characteristics which made them different from the surrounding nations and empires of their day, and they have suffered more than any other race in human history because of their unique identity. But they still exist. Hitler in Germany tried to exterminate them but failed.

The survival of the Jewish race defies all conventional wisdom, and when one adds that much of their history was foretold and that much of its future has been predicted in the Bible, it becomes an example of the intervention of some superior force or power acting for them. What we should recognize is that because the nation's future has been foretold, it cannot be defeated or destroyed.

We have already seen how they were established as a distinct nation, having begun life after the Flood as the descendants of Noah's son Shem. And then, as the 12 sons of Jacob, the grandson of Abraham, they travelled to Egypt as a total of 70 persons to escape the famine which was denuding their homeland. They then escaped from Egypt, after over 400 years of servitude, by a series of miraculous events, under the leadership of that most remarkable man Moses, by which time they probably numbered over 2 million persons. They then endured a further 40 years of journeying through desert and wilderness because of their unbelief and disobedience until they finally entered the land promised to their ancestor, Abraham. Now no longer simple pastoralists, they had the vital experience of living in a highly complex civilization, Egypt, and their leader, Moses, had been brought up and educated in the exclusive precincts of a royal palace. Moses, at the age of 40, had chosen to side with his persecuted people and had left his foster home to live for a further 40 years as a shepherd in the land of Midian. Before God called him by appearing as a burning bush.

Now began the two hundred years of conquest and occupation of the so-called 'Promised Land', that mountainous land of hills and fertile valleys occupied by a number of separate kingdoms, comprising the coastal area called Canaan, part of what later became known as Palestine and which was known at the time as the region of West Euphrates.

However, in the early years of their occupation, they were not yet a united nation, still living and warring as twelve tribes, and it was not until Saul became king that the tribes were finally united as one nation under one ruler, achieving its heights of military power under King David and then achieving enormous wealth and prestige under his son Solomon. This unity lasted roughly one hundred years because, after Solomon's death, the nation was divided into two separate nations. In the North were ten tribes under their king, Jeroboam, whilst the capital and centre of worship remained in the South, where the tribes of Judah and Benjamin remained loyal to David's memory.

There was then just a brief period before, in 722 BC, the Northern kingdom fell to the Assyrians, who were taking control of the area between the Euphrates and Egypt. The Southern kingdom suffered, particularly from the year 605, but remained intact until in 586/7 they too fell victims to an invader, this time the Babylonians, who had replaced the Assyrians as the major power in that region.

Once again, their remarkable story continues when, under the new power in the region, the Persians, who had overcome and replaced the Assyrians and the Babylonians, allowed the Hebrew people to return and, most amazingly, to rebuild both their capital city, Jerusalem, and their Temple for the worship of Almighty God. For the next 400 years, the nation continued to exist and survived the invasion of that area of West Euphrates by the Romans, who, in accordance with their political ideology, allowed Israel to be more or less self-governing. However, the unruly nature of that nation meant that they had to live under the supervision of successive governors appointed by Rome. That was the situation when Jesus of Nazareth was born, lived, and died and, according to his followers, was raised to life. The resurrection and subsequent ascent to heaven marked the beginning of what is today known as Christianity. A religious grouping, fundamentally based on the life and death of Jesus, who was Himself a Jew and was seen by His followers as the 'son of David', whose coming had been spoken of by their prophets as the one who would reign eternally as their king, but whom they rejected and killed. This situation only lasted for some thirty-five years after the time of Jesus, for, in AD 70, the Roman authorities, fed up with the rebellious nature of this self-governing province, attacked and captured Jerusalem and, as a final act, destroyed both the city and its Temple and exiled all its inhabitants.

This then began the two thousand years of exile for the Jewish nation, which, having begun under the Romans in AD 70, finally came to an end in May 1948 when, as Britain surrendered its mandate over the territory known as Palestine, the independent nation-state known as Israel came into existence once again. But did that end the persecution? Recent history answers that with a resounding NO. So what has happened since?

Today they are once again a unique and distinct nation with a complete history, dating back some 4,000 years, and their very existence after all these long years of trouble and testing is striking evidence both of the existence of their God, who foretold the whole thing, including what will happen in the future, and becomes evidence of the validity of the Jewish scriptures and the subsequent history of Christianity, which is rooted in Jewish history and whose very existence was foretold in the pages of the New Testament. But their story is far from over.

Some years ago, I was privileged to be invited to a conference at an American university in Oklahoma. In company with others, we flew to Paris, where we were joined by other guests from most of the European countries, and the following day we flew to New York and then on to Oklahoma, where we were met and taken to the University outside the city for the welcoming dinner, which was attended by a large number of obviously wealthy American citizens who appeared to be sponsoring the event.

During the three weeks of seminars and meetings, which occupied most of the time, we were also free to travel around. Transport was no problem as we were offered the free use of cars belonging to staff and senior citizens, who encouraged us to explore. Then, after dinner each evening, we attended a typical American mass rally with a number of speakers. In fact, I formed the conclusion that the university was holding a vast recruitment rally in the hope of expanding the number of other than American students, making it an international campus. This was very evident on the last night when we were asked to wear national costume. For me and for my fellow compatriots, no problem. British attire: a three-piece suit with a collar and tie. None of us had thought to pack a dinner jacket.

However, what amazed me was the great variety of 'national' costumes worn by our hosts. It began with a division, as they acknowledged, into those who 'met the boats' dressed in various native Indian attire and those who 'came over with the boats', meaning, of course, the settlers from Europe and many other countries who did their best to wear appropriate attire. But one significant factor that emerged from the assembly of our hosts was the number of nationalities who claimed Jewish descent, most of them having reached America whilst fleeing from persecution in their home countries.

In conversation during the evening, I found that many, many of these had fled persecution in countries as widespread as Russia, Asia, and central Europe and over a period of very many years. These were the fortunate ones who had prospered and become wealthy and were now actively engaged in helping their more recent 'cousins'.

Most of us will have either read of or seen the musical drama or at least be aware of the remarkable dramatic piece 'Fiddler on the Roof' set in Russia around the year 1905. It tells the story of a Jewish community suffering at the hands of the Russian police and ultimately being forced to emigrate to avoid persecution. In fact, it tells two stories. First, the way in which the milkman, the father figure, played by Chaim Topol, sees his family, especially his youngest daughter, marrying outside their faith and the pain, which that causes. The title was presumably taken from a painting by Marc Chagall, which features a violinist trying to play his violin whilst perched on the roof of his house. The Jewishness of this family was facing a dilution of faith through marriage whilst at the same time facing exile for their faith. A double dilemma.

Some nine years after my visit to the American University, I moved with my family some 70 miles east in order to take up a senior teaching post. Deciding not to live in suburbia, we bought an old house in the countryside. The original cottage was around 400 years old, the previous owners having modernized and extended it to provide relative luxury. However, our next-door neighbour, an elderly lady who, she told me, had taught French in the local school, was very interesting. Her large garden adjoined ours and it occupied much of her time, but she also loved to discuss ideas. Not political ones, but from literature and history.

She also showed us around her cottage, also modernized but only to the extent of providing modern facilities. However, as time passed, we began to discover more of her past. She showed us a painting of a very palatial residence, overlooking a lake, situated in what had been Prussia, and admitted that she had lived there with her husband and two sons. It turned out that her husband was a well-known sculptor whose work was on public display in Austria. In confidence she then told me that her husband had been friendly with Hitler and was one of his coterie of public figures, who included men like Max Schmeling, the boxer, who had been heavyweight World Champion in 1930–32 and achieved worldwide fame with his fights with Joe Louis in 1936 and 1938.

She now admitted that she had left her home in Austria and her husband because she disagreed with the principles of the Nazi party, and, facing the loss of all that prestige and privilege, she had left Germany in 1938 to come and live in England. However, knowing Gilda as well as I did, I accepted her statements at face value. It was not until after her death that I learned the truth.

Gilda had made me one of the trustees of her will, and, in perusing that, I discovered a very different story. Gilda had indeed been married to this famous sculptor and had lived with servants in some considerable style, but she had not left of her own volition. She was in fact a Jewess, married to an eminent Austrian who was closely associated with the German nationalistic party. Once this became public knowledge, she had been forced to leave because, as a Jewess, she was facing internment and had been very lucky to escape. Further, the marriage between her Aryan husband and herself, a Jewess, was deemed to have been irregular. I also discovered that, at least latterly, she had been receiving regular payments from her 'ex' husband and, further, when faced with a very expensive operation, the cost had been paid by none other than Max Schmeling, the boxer. Even more, her sons had obviously escaped with her, and one had been killed fighting against Germany as a pilot with the RAF. I met the younger son after his mother's death but was reluctant to press him for more information because he was in business in Italy. She was a very remarkable woman, but what a price she had had to pay, simply because of her Jewish birthright.

It was a fascinating account, and it explained much of what we had come to recognize. Although much was left unsaid and mystifying, it did account for what we saw of her life, which was not that of a financially impoverished teacher who had been teaching French in the UK. However, although I know her full name and that of her husband, I am reluctant to say more, because some of her relatives are still alive. I just wished that I had known more of her life as a Jewess whilst we lived as neighbours and could have heard the full story of her experience.

What we may well ask is why the Jewish faith has been so persistent, so satisfying, so life-changing that so many have been willing to pay the ultimate price rather than abandon their faith.

There are a number of factors regarding the longevity of the unique character of the Jews as a race, which we can consider. For example, the extraordinary way their belief has been transmitted. It originated with a direct encounter between human beings and God. But a God who was unique in that He claimed to be the creator of the whole of this mighty universe and said that there were no other gods. He alone was to be worshipped. This God interacted with, spoke to, and personally intervened in the lives of His followers. All other 'gods' were simply human expressions of what the human mind could invent or could define. Most of the religions from earliest times had 'gods' who originated from human ideas and were accepted in many different forms and guises but were all either not existing or were forms of demonic forces. Egyptians, for example, not only worshipped the sun and the river Nile, both being sources of fertility and life, but also predatory birds, the crocodile, and animals, each one in turn either producing material benefit or being embodied in earthly forms. Their pharaohs were seen as human versions of the gods. The Greeks had some 99 gods on Mars Hill in Athens plus an altar to the 'unknown' god, in case they had missed one out.

By contrast, the Jewish God was a spirit, creative, judgmental, righteous, and yet loving, but whose form could not be replicated, and any attempt to replicate Him was strictly forbidden because, as a spirit, He had no physical form, but, as with Adam and Eve and later others, He could communicate directly with the creature He had created. Further, He required worship in a clearly directed form with sacrificial offerings, as Adam's son Cain found out, and would severely punish any violation, as Cain found out when he killed his brother Abel in a fit of jealousy. The further implication being that the world was created as a good place, the Garden of Eden, but that evil was also present and trying to corrupt both the inhabitants and even nature itself to frustrate the purpose of God.

Possibly the most remarkable aspect of the Jewish God was that He not only spoke directly to humans but also made a series of covenants with them. These were all conditional, requiring obedience and discipline, but with great rewards and blessings attached for those who complied or pain and suffering, death and destruction, for those who ignored or failed to obey. However, above all else, their God had promised to give the nation a country exclusively their own, with a king, the descendant of their King David, whose rule in peace and equity would last forever. And that their nation and its king would rule the world. Isaiah 9:6–7. What they failed to understand was the concept of a suffering Messiah, as described in Isaiah chapter 53.

To this day the practicing Jews are daily awaiting, expecting, the return of their Messiah, at whose appearing the promises will finally be fulfilled and Israel, the nation, will rule the world, safe in its homeland, with its capital, Jerusalem, being the dwelling on earth of their God. And, even more remarkable, in support of this, Jewish history is filled with a series of miraculous events. Such as Noah and his family being saved from destruction by an ark. The twelve tribes, based on the twelve sons of Jacob, were delivered from their 400-year sojourn in Egypt by a series of plagues, the last of which involved the death of all first-born males, human or animal, but which did not touch the Israelites, whose children were spared because the people were told to kill a lamb, cook it, and eat it after sprinkling its blood on their doorposts and lintels. In the same way, when Pharaoh realized that his workforce had left, he pursued them, but his whole army was destroyed when they attempted to follow the Hebrews across the Red Sea as they walked; all 2 million of them plus their animals had crossed dry-shod.

But these were just two of the many miraculous events, which litter their history. The choice of leaders, the very detailed instructions for the construction of their temple, and all the elaborate ritual of their worship. And now, of course, the formation of the new national homeland in the very place which God had given to their founder, Abraham, and its current survival in the very perilous 20th century, where it is surrounded by countries which are opposed to it, particularly the Moslem areas, and the evidence of its ability to fight 'over its weight' in any encounters.

This idea had been reinforced over their history by dramatic or supernatural events, such as many years later after the construction of the tower named Babel, languages were diversified to prevent human people from challenging God. Then yet another dramatic sign, the destruction of the twin cities of Sodom and Gomorrah. God had warned Abram what was about to happen, and Abraham had pleaded for his nephew Lot, and finally God did agree that Lot was not a party to the sin of those cities that His angels had physically experienced. Abram, later renamed Abraham, was subjected to a number of tests. First telling him to leave the comfort of the relative security of a settlement, which was developing agriculture, situated to the east of the river Euphrates, and move westwards towards a new land which would become his future home and that of his descendants.

Abram and his wife Sarah were childless and both very elderly, so they were given a child supernaturally, and that child, named Isaac, was to become the progenitor of a new race of people. Abraham, as he now was, and his son, aged about sixteen, were now ordered to undergo a final and life-challenging test. A test so severe that it would potentially deny Abraham the promise of becoming the father of a great nation and that some of his descendants would become kings and ultimately that Jesus Christ was born into humanity as a descendant of Abraham.

It was because Abraham believed implicitly that God had promised that he would not only have illustrious descendants but also that he would, through them, become a blessing to the whole world that Abraham was able to trust God to find a solution to avoid disaster. So when Abraham was told by God to take his only son and sacrifice him on the mountain, known to us as Sinai, he did what God required. Totally confident that God would provide. So, setting off with servants on a three-day journey with wood and fire, the two of them left the servants and climbed the hill, but, saying as they left the immortal words, "Stay here with the donkey. The boy and I will go over there and worship, and then we will come back to you." Clearly Abraham believed that God would either bring his son back to life or provide an alternative. This was an absolute test of his faith in his God, in which Isaac must have shared, because he accepted his role without further challenge, not easy for a sixteen-year-old boy, but this experience must have been part of his own preparation for the future. Abraham found favour with God and was singled out by Him because of his absolute faith, confidence, and obedience.

The Jewish faith regards Abraham as its founding father for a number of reasons. Not least because God promised him that he would become the father of a great nation and that He would give to Abraham and his descendants a country of their own but also because God had promised to give them a king, who would be born into Abraham's family and be a descendant of King David. One whose dynasty would last forever, Isaiah 7:13–14.

No wonder then that even those of a cynical turn of mind have to marvel at the existence of this remarkable nation. But there is something even more remarkable about the Bible because if we examine it carefully, we find that it provides the answer to the biggest question of all. If, as the Jews and all Christians likewise believe, God created the universe (Genesis 1:1), a fact repeated several times and not just in Genesis (see John 1:1–3 and Colossians 1:16), then the issue becomes not 'how?' but 'why?' How? Becomes less important than the greater issue of why God went to all this trouble. Was there a purpose? And if so, what is it? No scientific exploration can answer that.

Chapter 4
Pre History

The Bible, the source of our information about the Jews, opens with an account of creation, which one can read as literally true or as an inspired account of the timeless creation of order and life out of a formless chaos. Science assumes that it began with a 'big bang', but they cannot explain where the constituent 'material' came from. Either way the creation story is there in the Bible because it teaches us a number of salient points. It teaches that creation is the action of a supreme omnipotent being, God, and not an accident of science. That into this creation, at the earliest moment of conscious thought, evil becomes present, and that this 'evil' will have consequences. We are told, in 2 Timothy 3:16, that "All scripture is inspired by God and is useful for teaching the truth, rebuking error, correcting faults, and giving instruction for right living." It therefore becomes a record of human existence in which every incident or every record is either literally true or, like a parable, is used symbolically to point out truth. The inspiration of scripture is that it is used by the Holy Spirit to teach us. Jesus, for example, taught spiritual truth in the form of parables, which often confused even His disciples, who needed to have them explained. Truth in God's terms is accessible only to those who seek the Truth. It is not found by the casual enquirer or those who are not sincere. Most religions have some form of explanation for the existence of the world. The three Abrahamic faiths, Jewish, Christian, and to a lesser extent the Muslim, all accept creation ex nihilo, i.e., out of nothing, by a supernatural being. Buddhists believe that the universe is self-recreating out of previous causes and is therefore impossible to define. The Greeks believed that Prometheus created mankind out of clay, the Norse that Odin and his brother created men out of trees, whilst the Sumerians look back to a great flood, with the survivors beginning afresh.

Human history then posits the development of a relationship between the creator and the created, made possible by a creator God's love, illustrated by the life, the death, and the subsequent resurrection of God's Son, who was sent into the world as a counterpoint to the failure of the first created beings, whose failure through human frailty would be redeemed by the loving mercy of God and by the presence of the Holy Spirit of God being made available to individuals.

Adam and Eve

We can say with some authority that the first couple mentioned in the Bible have been chosen for inclusion by the early compilers for a number of reasons, not necessarily because they were literally the first inhabitants of this blue planet. One of the reasons why they were picked out by the scribes who were looking back at the ancestral records must surely have been their symbolic significance. Yes, the Jewish scribes would have been aware of a number of other theories as to how it all began, but they were faced by a lack of other evidence, scientific or archaeological, which we, for many years, have had available in increasing depth. They required an answer which justified their own beliefs.

The early writers were endeavouring to establish certain facts, such as the idea that all of creation had its source in God. Then too they were exploring the origins of what later became known as 'sin' or evil and how such basic human factors became of religious or moral significance. In this case, an act which led to an act of disobedience to a direct command given by their God, whose presence in their lives had by this time been established. Only later would that act have been seen as a challenge to the authority of God.

However, a key issue in the account of Adam and Eve's early days, following their act of disobedience and the recital of their punishment, is found in Genesis 3:22. "And the Lord God said, 'Behold the man is become as one of us, to know good and evil'." The implication is that following their discovery of 'good and evil', they have become moral beings. Able to decide between what is right and what is wrong, it is this moral awareness, this responsibility, which distinguishes man from the wild beasts. I have dealt with this in much greater detail in my book, "The Kingdom of God."

Adam and Eve are not depicted as fully rounded creatures. There is no sense of personality and no character development. Hence their symbolic nature. The only real emotion which they show is Eve's pride and her risqué curiosity, which lays her open to the whispered temptation of wisdom, a choice offered by, in this case, a serpent who appears to have it. Adam can possibly be seen in a more favourable light in that his choice to follow Eve and accept the penalty, rather than lose his companion and the source of any offspring, by sticking to the commands of this God, may well suggest a sense of romantic attraction or even simply loyalty. Which we might well accept as a mark of his fondness for her, his love for a beautiful woman, as well as the practicality of not wanting to be alone. However, here they are created directly by God for a specific purpose, to multiply and replenish the earth, for we have been told that the universe, when first made, had no inhabitants and no vegetation. Their separation would have frustrated God's purpose in creation and, more importantly, it would have brought this new creation into the power of an alien force who, by that act, was challenging the authority of their creator. Accepting the offer put Eve in the serpent's power.

Symbolically this act opens up the major issue which will underlie the whole Bible. The existence of two forces. The good power, God the creator, and opposing Him an alien challenge which will do all in his power to disrupt and destroy God's creation until finally he is destroyed. He may simply be there to answer the question, 'Where did sin come from?' And to illustrate that this 'sin' was a human response to an external challenge, which arose from their very vulnerability as human beings. But he also exists, or is allowed to exist, to test the veracity of our allegiance to God. To test our faith and trust in God's love. And his final destruction, together with all his myriad followers, will demonstrate God's power, as in Armageddon. So, Adam and Eve are not simply stereotypes, and they may be seen as symbolic only in the sense that their dilemma is 'typical' of all humanity. In life we are all faced with having to make choices, and our response is dictated often by either our character or the circumstances of our situation, but its source is the presence of an alternative.

Then we read that they were 'made in His image', able to communicate with their creator, and set in a garden, with instructions to multiply and care for their environment, Genesis 2:15 and 1:28. So, apart from the introduction of 'days', creation could have followed the order suggested by modern science. However, humankind as described here was also given a moral sense because they were given a clear choice, that whilst they could eat of the fruit of any tree, there was one prohibition, an alternative. A tree from which they must neither touch nor eat. To do so would mean death, the end of their unique relation with their God, their spiritual life, the restoration of which would require what Jesus called a

"New Birth." To be born again of the Holy Spirit, as He told Nicodemus. John 3:16. The whole issue was brought about by the challenge to God's authority. "Did God really tell you not to eat the fruit from any tree in the garden?" Genesis 3:1. And it is that challenge to the authority of God's word which underlies all 'sin' described in the Bible.

So, right at the beginning we see God's creation and His authority being challenged by supernatural forces, and this will become a recurring theme throughout the whole book. But ultimately the issue is that of obedience to the word of God, who, as our creator, has the right to demand our allegiance. And this issue will become more and more important as the narrative progresses. See 1 Samuel 16:35 for the disobedience which cost King Saul his kingdom. Here the symbolism is completed by the prophetic words to the snake, "Her offspring will crush your head, and you will bite her offspring's heel." Genesis 3:15. And this refers to the death of Jesus, whose suffering on behalf of humankind would put an end to Satan's power and, by His resurrection, overcome the power which death has held for so long over the human race. And then the eternal, everlasting kingdom of God will be established. The hope of Jew and Gentile.

Eve and Adam then both disobey that initial command. They fail the test and incur the punishment, which is death. This is not physical death at this point but a spiritual death, which is shown in the loss of their personal relationship with God, who had previously 'walked' in the garden with them. The shame and fear which follow come from within them, their conscience. Once again this speaks to us symbolically of the fact that man was born to be in a relationship with his creator, hence 'made in the likeness of God'. The remedy for which, the ability to be in a close relationship with God, could only come when God, in the likeness of His Son Jesus, should take human form and pay the penalty on our behalf. Becoming, as Paul will later describe it as 'a second Adam'. Enabling us to 'die' in the person of Jesus on our behalf and to be 'born again', born of the Holy Spirit, as Jesus told Nicodemus in John 3:3–6.

So, whether the account of Adam and Eve is literally true or there as an allegory, it establishes the basic principles under which will develop a race known throughout the universe as 'the children of God'. This is further reinforced by God's immediate response, which is to warn the woman (3:16) of pain in childbirth and the man of hard work and toil to produce food (3:19). However, in mitigation and with a promise that would be fulfilled some 4,000 years later, God warned the snake that the 'seed of the woman', Jesus, would 'crush his head', destroy him. Genesis 3:18.

The next significant event, following the birth of two children, Cain and Abel, is the disastrous murder of Abel by his brother, and this is over the issue of whose 'offering to God' was acceptable. Cain, who brought an offering of his produce, or Abel, who brought a firstborn lamb. The record states that God was pleased with the offering of a lamb but rejected Cain's fruit of the fields, at which Cain was really angry, which implies that being acceptable to God was very important, even at this stage of their development. Again, this is very significant because it is the first clear indication that the Creator God required, demanded, obedience and also worship and that worship required a blood sacrifice, which will later be codified under the leadership of Moses.

In response, God banished Cain, removing him from further contact with his family, and marked him to prevent him from being killed. In this context one could also argue that he was removed to prevent his attitudes from corrupting his immediate family. Cain then marries a wife, and when a son was born to them, he established a city. We are then given a list of the descendants of Cain. This is highlighted because after that Cain's children are not named because they have been excluded from the 'chosen seed'. However, to continue what we might define as the 'god line', Adam and Eve do have another son, whom they name Seth, and it is through Seth that the true bloodline continues. Cain's descendants are ignored but not forgotten, for they will appear later in our story, so that in Genesis Ch 5:1 it is only Adam's children from Seth who are recognized, and this is later repeated in 1 Chronicles 1:1–4, where again Cain's bloodline is ignored.

Noah

Now comes a monumental statement in Genesis Ch. 6 when we are told that sometime later, when the human race had spread over all the world, the wickedness mankind is capable of had increased and, most particularly, was now seen in the union of beautiful earth-born women with angelic beings. Which gives rise to or becomes the source of a race of giants, the Anakim, mentioned again when the Israelites begin their conquest of Canaan and also potentially men of renown, 'the great heroes and famous men of long ago'. There has even been a suggestion that what we call 'genius' is in fact a God-given gift. But there is no time evidence here; we are just told that evil becomes so rampant, as Jude will also comment, in Jude verse 6, that God regrets having created humanity and determines to wipe it all out and begin again, Genesis 6:5–7, which He did, with one man, Noah, who, the evidence suggests, had not been contaminated by all this 'evil'. 2 Peter 2: 5 "God did not spare the ancient world but brought the Flood on the world of godless people. The only people He saved were Noah, who preached righteousness, and seven other people." Here in the Psalms is further evidence: "The Lord looks down from Heaven at human beings to see if there are any who are wise, any who worship Him. But they have all gone wrong; they are all equally bad. Not one of them does what is right. Not one of them." Psalm 14:2–3. And yet another piece of evidence mentioned by Peter, relating to the existence of angelic forces which are evil. As opposed to those who are the servants of God. "God did not spare the angels who sinned but threw them into Hell, where they are kept chained in darkness, waiting for the day of Judgement." 2 Peter 2:4.

Noah appears less of an individual and more of a typical example, or a symbol. His chief or most important characteristic being that he 'believed'. In other words, he trusted in what he believed to be something that had been conveyed to him. There is no debate, no emotional reaction, no having to come to terms with the enormity of the task he was set, and no description of the actual construction of the enormous vessel. He believed, and he acted in obedience to what he had been given. Even though at the time there was no other evidence to show that what he was doing was right. All we know about this from historical and apocryphal evidence is that at that time old records indicate that there was a flood in that area and that other mythological records describe the construction of a very large vessel, complete with details of how to construct it. Were the priests, writing later, using this known data to illustrate a point? To illustrate what later would become known as 'faith'. Belief in something for which there was no physical evidence. But once again we are being introduced to the 'why' of creation. That God is preparing for something even greater but is being opposed at every stage by evil forces.

However, the flood and the elimination of all unacceptable persons lead to two things. First, we are told that after the birth of Seth's son, whom he named Enosh, 'people began using the Lord's holy name in worship' (Genesis 4:26). Which in itself suggests that knowledge of God, that is, God the creator of the universe, was becoming increasingly known. This was a time when most cultures worshipped gods of their own making. Invented or 'created' out of a superstitious imagination, or was a way of explaining those things that at that time were otherwise inexplicable. Secondly, amongst the apparent evil of much of that period, certain names stand out as being acceptable by this supernatural creator God, one of whom, mentioned in the past, as a descendant of Adam's son Seth, was Enoch (Genesis 5:21–24) who did not die but was 'taken away' by God. Amongst the other named persons was Enoch's great-grandson Noah, who, as we have just seen, was called a preacher of righteousness and whose father was Lamech and whose grandfather was Methusaleh. This was a very distinguished ancestry, and it was Noah of whom at birth it was said, "From the very ground on which the Lord has put a curse, this child will bring us relief from all our hard work." And this was the man whom God selected to begin the 'human race' over again by enabling him and his immediate family, plus representative members of all the animals, to escape from a disastrous and totally destructive flood. and begin again with Noah's three sons.

The remarkable thing about this man Noah, of whom we know so little except his illustrious ancestry and that we are told that he was a "just man and walked with God," is that he was an individual who was able to communicate with God. Presumably by a vision, and that he had the temerity, the faith, and the vision to construct a large vessel on dry land in anticipation of an event that would have been totally outside of his knowledge. Once again, as we shall find repeatedly, the people who were to become the 'children of God' were singled out for their willingness to respond so positively to this otherwise unknown God, leading to their obedience to a specific command and warning them of pending disaster.

Historically and geologically, there is evidence of a disastrous flood which took place at some time in the past when the area in Southern Mesopotamia along which run the two great rivers which flow into the Red Sea, the Tigris and the Euphrates, was engulfed by water from the Persian Gulf, possibly as far up as Mt. Ararat in modern Turkey. And this is borne out by other accounts of a similar occurrence recorded in other literature of the period. Werner Keller, in his book 'The Bible as History', refers to manuscripts discovered in the late 19th and early 20th Century in the ancient city of Nineveh, the capital city of Syria, most particularly a series of clay tablets which contained accounts of an ancient king, the Epic of Gilgamesh, which refer to an ancient story which is very similar to the one referred to in the book of Genesis. Of a man who was told to build a large boat to escape a major flood. These and about 20,000 other clay tablets were found in the ancient library at Nineveh, which was one of the most famous in the ancient world. Here, in the Biblical version, it is used to illustrate the idea of a people who would in time become known as the 'children of God', whose history proved not only that their God was greater than the gods of other nations but that He was singling out a race who would serve His purpose on earth, which was to demonstrate His love and His power.

A further example lies in the fact that, clearly, there is a lengthy period between the end of Chapter 5 and the ideas portrayed in Chapter 6. There are no means by which we can identify each period because there are no known contemporary features mentioned other than the sparse details of the state of civilization revealed in the text. And, as these details would have been constructed at a much later date because no written records were available at the time, the writers may well have used features which were contemporary with the time of writing and the expectation of their time.

If so, then the narrative now continues with the descendants of Noah, not because all the rest of the world's inhabitants were drowned but because the lineage of which the Bible is concerned was now based on persons acceptable to God. Acceptable because of their ability to or willingness to 'believe' in Him. This idea is expressed in the words of scripture, 'These are the descendants of Noah's sons, Shem, Ham, and Japheth'. Genesis 10:1. Any or all of the other peoples who would have been alive at the time are excluded. Making this exclusive history, not an inclusive one. Even though the record states 10:12. All these peoples are the descendants of Noah, nation by nation, according to their lines of descent. After the flood all the nations of the earth were descended from the sons of Noah.

The elaborate detail of construction and of eight persons and the number of animals taken into the Ark having to be sustained with food and water for the time given, 40 days of rain, 150 days of the flood, 150 days of the water going, and then a further 40 days before the earth had dried out, a period of ten months before the tops of the mountains appeared at 8:5, makes this an event which would have been seen as miraculous.

The Tower of Babylon

The story of the Tower of Babylon Genesis 11 refers to the people of the whole world having only one language and says that 'they' came to a plain in Babylonia, an area between the rivers Euphrates and Tigris, and settled there. We also know that at the time of Abraham there were elaborate civilisations existing not only in the Middle East but also elsewhere, the remains of which are being discovered and dated by current archaeological exploration.

However, if this was a localized event which devastated a certain area occupied by the people to whom we have been introduced, then it is both feasible and a useful analogy or metaphor for the result of sin. For the real history of the 'children of God' begins not with Noah but with Abraham, who is introduced in chapter 12 as the descendant of Shem, one of Noah's sons (Genesis 11:10).

Because these events occurred before writing was available, the earliest forms were the Sumerian wedge-shaped cuneiform impress on clay tablets and the Egyptian hieroglyphics; these earliest records would have been constructed later as written parchments. But recent historical and geographical discoveries are increasingly uncovering more and more evidence from the Middle East and especially of the fertile Crescent of Mesopotamia right up to what is now modern Turkey and as far as the Nile valley in Northern Egypt are uncovering names and places made familiar in the Bible. All of which makes it possible that the later writers from the priesthood were using the mythology which appears in several early cultures to provide graphic pictures of the origins of sin and its consequences to provide a metaphorical record. Certainly, these early figures are not developed as characters, being depicted as static figures on an ideal landscape; in other words, they may have been symbolic representations drawn from local culture.

On the other hand, as modern science is tending towards the recognition that creation may have been brought about by a vastly high intelligence, the God of the Bible, these events may have their source in fact. Either way, whether they are historically accurate or symbolic representations, they are part of the inspired word of God and are therefore profitable for instruction in righteousness. They are valuable to us, either as history or as instructive statements.

Chapter 5
The Patriarchs

Abraham First Called Abram

Historically, the account of the Israelite nation begins with the arrival on the scene of Abram, who will later be described as the father of the nation and renamed Abraham. At this point, we become aware that the events are far more detailed and can, in many cases, be identified timewise from contemporary records outside of the scriptural record. Because we have historical and geological evidence to support it. For example, the city of Ur was a Sumerian city which has now been explored by archaeologists, and the lifestyle of families like that of Abraham are detailed in their records. The area of fertile land which lay between the river Nile to the west and the Euphrates and Tigris rivers in the east, the land between the rivers, has been described as the cradle of civilization with evidence of established cities and cultivation with records going back some 3,500 years B.C. There is evidence of several cities built of sun-dried mud and with towers called ziggurats, built, it is assumed, to honour their gods. It is most likely that one of these is being described in Genesis 11:4–9 at a city which became known as Babylon, archaeological evidence for which still exists because it was developed into a major city and became the capital city of that area. The Sumerians, who occupied that area, are also known for having created a system of writing using wedge-shaped blocks, and it is from these that we can develop a picture of their lifestyle and achievements. This was the area which we know as Mesopotamia. The other civilization of that era and area was to be found around the lower Nile, in what became known as Egypt, and we know from their records that they were an advanced civilization constructing large monuments out of stone and with a large military force, which made them a formidable entity with powerful rulers. We also know that they had quite remarkable skills, having considerable medical ability and a knowledge of anatomy derived from their use of mummification for burying their dead. They had devised a calendar based on the solar system, discovered the use of bronze, a mixture of copper and lead, and devised a system of writing which developed into what we call hieroglyphics. As a result, they left a number of texts describing their daily lives and giving us a record of their religious beliefs, which included their belief in an afterlife. We know that some of their early monuments date back to around 2,600 BC, and many of these monuments are still there today, much more significant than the Sumerian heritage.

The land, which would become known as Canaan and which became the destination of the nation founded by Jacob's sons, was situated between these two great civilisations. It was a land of contrasts, of mountains and valleys, watered not by the great rivers but by rain-forming streams and rivers, of which the best known was the river Jordan with its deep valley falling to nearly 3,000 feet below sea level at the area which became known as the Dead Sea, forming its eastern boundary and creating a natural border for this fertile land.

It is therefore reasonable for us to say that Abraham lived some 2,000 years before the time of Christ because from shortly after his lifetime, the chronology of the Bible becomes tied to other events and persons associated with them and whose timelines are linked to other known historical figures. We also know, from Biblical records, that Abraham was a nomadic tribesman at a time when 'civilisation' in Mesopotamia was quite advanced, in that cities and communities were being formed and constructed, as the archaeological evidence from this period demonstrates. Just as later, when Jacob's children go down into Egypt, they will encounter a very highly developed culture, as again we have the evidence from archaeological excavation and restoration. Abraham's character is quite clearly defined for us. First he was a direct descendant of Noah through his son Shem, his father being Terah, who had three sons: Abram, Nahor, and Haran. Haran died in his native city of Ur in Babylonia. Terah then took his grandson Lot, the son of Haran; his son Abram; and Abram's wife Sarai, his daughter-in-law, and left their home in Ur to go to the land of Canaan. On the way there they reach Haran, a small city, and settle there, becoming very prosperous as sheep and cattle herders, and it was there that Terah would die at age 205 years.

Many years later, when Abram was 75 years of age, Abram received a direct message from a God who was unlike any other known at the time, and this God told him to leave their father's home, where they had become settled and very wealthy in animals and slaves, set out into what was an unknown land, and travel to a new country in which he will become the father of a great nation; even more propitious, God promised to bless him, make him famous, and through him, God would bless all the nations of the world. Genesis 12:3. Even more important, and with great consequences for the future, God said that He would bless those who were good to him and curse those who opposed him, a prediction which has echoed down the centuries since and still marks out his descendants as a unique group, hated by many but whose financial success has made them an important part of modern society, even whilst they were, for nearly two thousand years, exiled and without a national home.

When Abram and his family and all their children, slaves, and goods arrived in Canaan, they stopped first at a place named Shechem, where Abram made a sacrifice to God. They then moved to settle between Bethel and Ai before moving gradually further south, presumably looking for pasture for their substantial number of animals. They were a nomadic group, not settled in a city or enclosing land for agricultural farming.

Unlike Mesopotamia or Egypt with their large and strong rivers, which regularly flooded, providing a vast area of alluvial deposits, which were extremely fertile, the land of Canaan was well watered but depended on rainfall to feed the pastures from streams and smaller rivers. They were dependent on rain. Inevitably, after a while, there was a severe drought, and Abram was forced to move further south into Egypt to take advantage of the waters of the Nile Estuary, ironically a place where many generations later they would spend over 400 years in slavery. So, in obeying God's call to move to Canaan, Abram was becoming more and more dependent on God for directions and help. However, when they moved into that new area, with very many different societies all with their own cultures, each with its depravity and its worship of many different gods, Abram, to defend his wife, who was very beautiful, from predators, told her to say that she was his sister, which in fact she was. As a result, Sarai was taken by the king into the palace, and the result of that was an outbreak of a terrible disease. But in the meantime, the king had rewarded Abram richly, presumably with the intention of taking Sarai as his wife. So, the king sent for Abram, and when he heard the truth, he told Abram in anger to take his wife and leave immediately. Actually, Sarai was his sister, his father's daughter by a different mother. But the real issue is that Abram failed to trust God, and we have then a first instance of a curse, which God had said would afflict those who were unhelpful to Abram and later the Jewish nation. Abram now returns to Canaan a very rich man, and he and his nephew Lot moved back into the south of the land and camped again at the place where he had been before, an area between Bethel and Ai. Here Abram and Lot finally separated, simply because their flocks were too large to be pastured close together, and, given the choice, Lot chose the fertile Jordan valley, whilst Abram stayed in the hill country.

Sometime after this, four kings from Babylonia set out to capture five kings of the Jordan Valley, where Lot was living. This was at the time a routine action as each of the local communities was seeking to expand their territory and remove any possible threat from their neighbours. Ultimately the valley kings were defeated, some of their armies being trapped in the local tar pits. The four kings then ransacked the defeated cities and took all the loot, including Lot and all his possessions. When Abram heard the news, he set out with all his armed servants and sons and rescued Lot, defeating these four kings and bringing back all his nephew's family and possessions.

On his return, Abram was met by a local, Melchisedek, king of Salem, to whom he gave one tenth of all the loot he had recovered. Melchisedek is a unique character but extremely significant in Jewish lore. He is said to have had no parents and no recorded end to his life yet; Abraham paid him a tithe of all he had gained from the defeat of the four kings. This indicated that he was of higher rank than Abram and was regarded as a precursor of the role of High Priest, later to be played by Moses' brother Aaron before and after the Law was given under Moses, when ultimately the High Priest was chosen from the tribe of Levi, one of Jacob's sons.

It is shortly after this that God appears to Abram in a vision in which God makes a covenant with him (Genesis 15) in which He promises Abram two things. First, that the childless and aging Abram will have descendants as numerous as the stars in the sky and, second, that He will give him as his possession the whole of the land from the borders with Egypt to the River Euphrates. He also forecast that these descendants of his will be treated cruelly for 400 years but escape with great wealth. Abram believed what God had told him, and it was this belief here and later which marked him out as a man accepted by God. It was because of his complete faith in God that future generations would look back and regard him as the father of their nation. It was this implicit faith, which enabled him to become the great man, which God had promised.

It appears that Abram, in spite of his initial trust in a God who told him to leave home and establish himself in a foreign country, which was inhabited by strong forces, is being tested in his experiences. Preparing him for greater tests ahead. Abram is seen from his earliest years and, in spite of his very human failures, to have been very responsive to the influence of this new God who, unlike the gods of the surrounding nations', was able to communicate directly with him; the problem was that he had no child. On his death all his property would pass to his chief steward. His wife, a very beautiful woman who was his half-sister, was, like most women of the time, totally submissive to her husband and accepted her role as being important. However, she was childless, and this, to a very rich man like Abram, was a perpetual problem. Most especially because at this time his God was telling him that he was to become the father of a large family, which would become a great nation. His wife's solution was to have a child by her maid, Hagar, and indeed Abram did this, and a child was born, Ishmael. But once again, this lack of total trust in his relationship with his God would result in that child becoming a major problem, as he became the progenitor of the tribal itinerants named Ishmaelites.

Sometime after this, when he was 99 years old, Abram's God appeared to him again and renewed the covenant and renamed him Abraham because he would become the father of a nation and gave him the sign of the covenant, which was that Abraham and all his descendants should be circumcised. Following this, God appeared to him again as he sat at his tent door in the heat of the day and promised him that he would have a son by Sarah, his wife. Sara, listening from the tent, just laughed because not only was she old and well past childbearing, but Abraham was now nearly 100 years old. As an interlude at this point, we are given a very dramatic example of the increasing intensity of the relationship between Abraham and his God when the Lord tells him that the city where his nephew Lot is living is to be destroyed and Abraham pleads with God to spare the city. However, only Lot and his two daughters finally escape, Lot's wife, having looked back, was turned into a pillar of salt. Interestingly, recent archaeological exploration has determined that there was an atomic explosion found in the rocks. Just as is the case with Mt. Carmel, where Elijah's fire burnt up the stones as well as the sacrifice.

Now we find that just as promised, Sarah did have a child whom they named Isaac, and as the two children grew, Sarah became increasingly concerned that Hagar's child would deprive her son Isaac of his father's wealth, and she tormented Hagar until Hagar ran away with her child and left him under a bush as she prepared to die of hunger and thirst. However, in full justice, an angel appeared who rescued the mother and child, and he later grew to become the leader of a tribe, which would present serious problems for Abraham's son Isaac.

As if all this was not enough trouble for Abraham, when the child was about 16 years of age and his father well over 100, Abraham was told to make the ultimate sacrifice, one which was quite common amongst the pagan nations. He was told to take his only son, his hope for the future, and to sacrifice him to God as a proof of his faith in God, even though potentially the way in which God's promise that he would become the father of a great nation would be fulfilled had to be through Isaac. So we see the two of them, the old man and his young son, setting out, leaving the servants as they climbed Mt. Moriah. Isaac, asking where the sacrifice was, was simply told that God would provide, and he did. As Abraham raised his knife to complete the sacrifice, he was stopped by an angelic voice, and there caught by its horns in a thicket was a ram. And this ram took the place of the child.

A harrowing story, yes, but the sublime test of Abraham's faith in his God, which would in future generations be seen symbolically as a projection, a foretelling of the greater sacrifice by God of His only Son, as He died, the sacrificial lamb, to take our place in order to redeem us from our mortality brought about by disobedience. Hence, the emphasis in our Lord's prayer in the garden of Gethsemane on His acceptance of His Father's will. "Let this cup pass from Me; nevertheless, not My will but Thy will be done." The final act of total obedience is as Jesus surrenders Himself to the awful horror of a Roman crucifixion, which was a personal and very public act of utter humiliation.

It was these acts of commitment and surrender to the will of God, which marked Abraham's life and made him the example to his descendants of conduct, which was both acceptable to God and made him one of God's sons. A blessing subsequently passed to his descendants, who became known as the sons of God. Whilst Abraham may appear as an austere example of a very rich man who had the command and respect of his family and servants, who obeyed his instructions without question, yet he was also a person who was not just responsive to God but shared a common vision of what God was doing with His creation. He was also a visionary who was looking to the future. Paul the apostle will later point out that in leaving the established civilization of the Chaldean neighbourhood of the well-established and developed city of Ur, Abraham was a man who shared a vision of a greater future than could be understood in simple earthbound terms. As Paul describes it, "He sought a city which hath foundations, whose builder and maker was God." Hebrews 11:10.

Abraham had two sons born to him, named Ishmael and Isaac. The first, by Hagar, his concubine, and named Ishmael, was destined to be blessed by God and become the father of a nation by virtue of his parentage, as we read in Genesis 21:13. Ironically, his descendants, listed for us in Genesis 25:12–18, would become a problem for the descendants of Isaac, as we shall later discover. This was because he was born of human endeavour and not by supernatural means. Whereas Isaac was born to parents, one of whom, Sarah, was too old for the natural process, which meant that even before his birth he was destined to have a specific purpose, which was the fulfilment of God's promise to Abraham that he would become the father of a great nation. But a nation which would continue and develop along the lines of his father Abraham; further evidence of the way in which, during the development and growth of the population of the earth at this time, we can see that certain persons were being singled out by God, uniquely chosen, for a purpose which at this time was not evident. And each of these early chosen persons would encounter God, or a representative of God, which would mark them out as 'different'.

Isaac

As our story continues with this 'special' Isaac, the first thing we observe is that before Abraham finally dies at a ripe old age of 175, Sarah having died already aged 127, he arranges for his oldest servant to find a wife for Isaac. He is told to vow in the most strict manner not to let Isaac marry from amongst the local Canaanites because this would break the unique relationship with Abraham's God. Genesis 24:3–4, This care in selecting marriage partners was intended to keep the 'bloodline' pure, and we shall later see the disastrous effects which followed multiple marriages, most particularly in the arranged marriages between kings families to create a bond of friendship between nations, as with Solomon's marriage to the daughter of the king of Egypt. Therefore it was very important now for them to seek his bride from amongst their relatives, and this too is a case of the servant seeking God's guidance as he travels all the way back to their former home in Mesopotamia, where he sits by a well and prays that God will answer his prayer by showing him which of the young women was to be Isaac's wife. Genesis 24:11–27. This is the beginning of a love story which would rank high in the history of romantic marriages, not just in the sense of God taking a personal interest in human affairs, but also as another example of the way in which those old 'Abraham's sons, because they, centuries later, embraced the same special relationship were keen to protect and preserve their bloodlines'. This 'special' relationship required a full and total commitment from the recipients. This was not an imposed order but, right from the beginning, involved a cooperation, an awareness of the fact that this relationship existed. How remarkably this lays the basis for the New Testament level of commitment required, first in the disciples of Jesus and later in the new converts who would be comprised of people from all nations, both of Jewish heritage and non-Jewish who, in becoming the 'sons of God', came into that relationship by means of what Jesus called a 'new birth' John 3:3. This extension of the race of chosen ones even led to them being called the 'sons of Abraham' repeatedly in the New Testament.

Isaac was in fact 40 years old at the time of his marriage to Rebecca, who was described in the text as being very beautiful. She too accepts her role and is prepared to go with the servant without question. Even though her brother and her mother wanted to delay her acceptance. The question was put to her, and her immediate answer was 'yes'. Genesis 24:58.

It is quite clear that Isaac loved Rebecca, because we are told, after his marriage, that he was comforted for the death of his mother, and, we subsequently learn, his father also died and was buried by the two sons in the cave in which Abraham had buried his wife, Sarah. Which implies that by this time the two brothers were, if not reconciled, at least not in conflict. We are also reminded in Genesis 25 that apart from Abraham's marriage to Hagar, he also had, as was the custom in those days, another wife named Keturah, by whom he also had further sons. However, although out of his very considerable wealth he had made provision for those 'other' sons, the bulk of his wealth still went to Isaac, the son of promise.

Then follows a genealogical list of the descendants of Ishmael, whom we shall encounter later because they will become antagonistic to the chosen race and will be one of those nations which will oppose and create problems for their relatives. A situation which will continue through to Isaac and his descendants, even though they occupy a very different area of land near Egypt, which is where generations later they will oppose the passage of the nation of Israel (Abraham's sons) after their escape from slavery in Egypt and head for Canaan, which was to become their home.

Returning to the story of Isaac and Rebecca, we are told of a very significant development, the birth of their first two sons, twins named Jacob and Esau. The importance of this lies in the fact that although Esau was born first, he does not value his birthright and sells it to Jacob for a bowl of stew, and by so doing he forfeits his place in the unique line which is developing. The story, which is told in greater detail later, shows how events seen at the time as relatively unimportant can ultimately have enormous consequences. Esau now further compounds his own problems by marrying two Hittite women, Judith and Basemath, who, we are told, made life miserable for Isaac and Rebecca.

Then comes a rather startling development. Isaac is getting old and has become blind. The time has therefore arrived for him to officially declare his intentions for his descendants, and that meant giving his blessing to his eldest son as his heir. Rebecca hears him telling Esau to go out and get some of his favourite meat, cook it, and bring it to him, and then he would give him his final blessing. In spite of everything, Esau was his favourite son because he was an outdoorsman, a hunter, and one who provided his father with the venison that he loved to eat. And, of course, he did not know that Esau had 'sold' his birthright to Jacob, but their mother knew and took Jacob's side. Together they played a trick on both Esau and Isaac. Instructing him how to disguise himself as his hairy brother and by cooking Isaac's favourite food, Jacob took his brother's place and 'stole' the blessing. Returning later after a successful hunt, Esau goes to his father for the blessing only to find that Jacob has taken it. He is seriously angry, and his father is deeply disturbed, but the deed cannot be undone. Rebecca, realizing the potential consequences, sends Jacob away to her brother Laban, living in Haran, Mesopotamia. Isaac supports this, telling Jacob not to marry a Canaanite woman and agreeing with his wife. Esau's choice of Hittite wives had actually angered Isaac. Realising this as one reason for losing the eldest son's blessing, Esau then goes and marries a daughter of the rejected Ishmael. We can see how the odds here are stacked in favour of the 'chosen' one from each generation. The others not being aware that through each generation a 'plan' was evolving, which would be revealed many generations later. And we have not seen the last of Esau.

Jacob

Now back to Jacob as he travels from Beersheba, heading back to Mesopotamia from whence his grandfather had set out at the call of God so long ago. It is now that Jacob has his first recorded encounter with his grandfather's God, in a remarkable dream of a ladder reaching from earth to heaven and with angels going up and coming down, and with it he saw the Lord. Note that the angels here were based on earth, going back up to heaven before returning to earth. The Lord, the God of Abraham and Isaac, then tells him that He will give him the land on which he is lying, that He will bless him with numerous descendants, and will bring him back to this place and never leave him until all these things have happened.

Jacob is both amazed and afraid, saying this must be "the house of God; it must be the gate that opens into heaven." Genesis 28:17.

What is so remarkable about this incident is that it illustrates the way in which God is accepting this man who has not been totally honest as the rightful heir of his grandfather Abraham by repeating the original promise made to Abraham. God's plan is unfolding or developing through far from perfect human channels. As Paul will later add, "We have this treasure in earthen vessels that the excellence of the power might be of God and not of man." 2 Corinthians 4:7.

Arriving at his uncle's home, Jacob meets and falls in love with his cousin, Rachel, and agrees to serve for seven years as the 'bride price'. However, now is the turn for Jacob to be deceived as Laban substitutes Leah, the elder sister, for his beloved Rachel and is forced to serve for a further seven years to pay for Rachel, a time which he calls nothing because of his great love for Rachel. Sadly, Rachel is barren, and it is Leah who provides Jacob with children. Rachel. even gives Jacob her slave Bilhah, who bore him two sons. Leah, then past childbearing, also gives Jacob her slave Zilpah, and finally God relents and allows Rachel to bear two sons, first Joseph and then, dying in childbirth, she bears a second son, Benjamin.

Between these four women, Jacob fathers twelve sons, vitally important because they will become the twelve fathers of the embryonic nation of Israel. However, after the birth of Joseph, Jacob realizes that it is time to leave Haran and return to his own family now living in part of what will become their inheritance. However, Laban has not finished with Jacob, and we are told how even after Jacob had served for 14 years for his two wives, Laban's daughters, Laban now attempts to cheat him of his wages. However, with God's help, Jacob outwits Laban and leaves a very prosperous and wealthy man, and he is finally reconciled with his uncle, and they make an agreement of friendship and cooperation at a place called Mizpah before he sets out to meet his brother Esau as he returns.

However, anticipating problems, he stops to send messengers ahead to his brother. At the same time he is met by some angels and, having been warned by the messengers that his brother is coming with a strong force of men. Jacob prays most earnestly to his Grandfather Abraham's God, and, in a most remarkable account, we hear that he wrestled in prayer with one of the angels, who is actually forced to disable him in order to escape from the struggle and smites him on his hip. Jacob asks the 'man' for his name only to be told that having successfully struggled with God and with men and won, he would be renamed Israel. Jacob names the place Peniel, saying, "I have seen God face to face, and I am still alive."

What a singular experience and what a demonstration of the way in which God was both selecting his chosen ones and personally guiding them. Who this angelic man was is open to question, but it was a remarkable incident and certainly a miraculous one, which can be taken as a symbolic representative of what prayer sometimes involves.

Although Jacob was very nervous, afraid even, of the meeting with his brother Esau, to such an extent that he divided his party up into groups, sending forward a valuable collection of sheep and cattle as a gift. However, when they do meet, Esau appears friendly and offers to escort him back to his home place. Jacob, fearful that his wealth, comprising large flocks, would cause friction or jealousy, certainly finding pasture for such a number as had happened generations earlier with his grandfather Abraham and his nephew Lot would have been a problem had the two brothers lived in proximity. So, under the guise of a slow pace to avoid stressing the animals and even his own children, Jacob wisely decides to make his home at first at a place called Sukkoth before finally settling in the land of Canaan, where he bought land from a man named Shechem. Some distance away from Esau, who had returned to his home in the land of Edom. Which is where we shall later find them, and by their attitude and their actions towards Jacob's descendants, we will see that the enmity between the brothers was still an active factor, causing considerable problems for what would become the nation of Israel. Jacob had been renamed by the angel at Peniel.

The last time we see the two brothers together is recorded in Genesis 35:27–29 when they go to Mamre near Hebron to bury their father, Isaac, who had died at the ripe old age of 180 years. We are then told that Esau and his descendants became the nation of Edom, a nation which had had kings as rulers long before the idea of kings became an issue in the nation of Israel. 1 Chronicles 1: 43–54, and we shall later discover how deep-seated that enmity was as Edom, the nation, becomes a problem for the nation of Israel.

The history of Jacob now becomes the history of the nation of Israel, and we encounter a number of defining incidents, beginning with his twelve sons. Of them, Jacob's two youngest sons born to his beloved wife Rachel were his favourites, Joseph and Benjamin, with Joseph being singled out when his father had a special long-sleeved robe made for him. However, this favouritism led to jealousy, which was compounded by his always reporting to his father the bad behaviour of the older sons, and it came to a head when he had two dreams. The first told of a field of wheat sheaves bowing down to him and then a second in which the sun, the moon, and eleven stars bowed to him. At the time Joseph was only 17 years of age, and his brothers and even his father were outraged. However, this was the first sign that Joseph had been singled out for a unique future in which he would play a vital part in the future of the whole family, but a remarkable future which would only come after a period of intense suffering. Once again, as with his great-grandfather Abraham, what was happening was to become a foretelling of the way in which God would deliver humanity from the slavery of sinful disobedience.

Joseph

Sent by his father to go and find his brothers who were living with their flocks and herds of animals as they travelled to find fresh pasture, his brother decided to punish him. The first idea was to kill him, but it ended with Joseph being sold to travelling Ishmaelite traders who in turn sold him as a slave to an Egyptian army commander. Here we see a very different Joseph. No longer the arrogant spoiled child, he becomes a very much valued servant in the household until the commander's wife falls in love with him, and when he rejects her advances, she accuses him of attempted rape, and he is thrown into prison. Here too, his behaviour makes him a favourite with the jailor, who, like the army commander, gives him a position of authority. Now back to dreams, and this time Joseph correctly reads the dreams of Pharaoh's two servants, his butler and his baker. Reading the dreams correctly, Joseph foretells the promotion and reinstatement of the butler and the death of the baker. The butler forgets Joseph for some time until the Pharaoh has a dream which greatly troubles him, and only then does he remember the vital part which Joseph had played in understanding the meaning of his dream in prison. Sent for, Joseph presents himself before Pharaoh and immediately is able to understand the significance of Pharaoh's two dreams, which predicted a seven-year period of bountiful harvests followed by seven years of disastrous famine. Egypt, at this time in its history, had become an extremely wealthy country and, as the rediscovered monuments now disclose, it was technologically advanced beyond any of its competitors, with much of its wealth being derived from the fertility of the river Nile.

Pharaoh and his advisors accepted the validity of Joseph's predictions, seeing him as a man who had the Spirit of God in him. Genesis 41:37. The result was that Joseph's plan of storing food during the years of plenty and being able to sell it during the famine was adopted, and it became the means of saving not only the Egyptian nation but some of the neighbouring countries as well.

All of this had taken many years, and the 17-year-old Joseph would now have been in his thirties. His brothers had explained the absence of Joseph, whom they had sold, by dipping his robe in animal blood and telling their father, Jacob, that Joseph must have been attacked by wild animals. Jacob had believed them and mourned deeply for his lost son. Now, some twenty years later, that teenage dreaming boy has become second in command in the great Egyptian empire. And the reason was simply that in God's great plan he, Joseph, was to play a vital part in the development of the tribe through events which would turn it from a tribe of some 75 people into a nation numbering some 2,000,000 people, which in turn would become one of the great nations of its day, wealthy, strategically placed on the fabled silk route, and militarily more powerful than its neighbours. All because they were promoted and empowered by their God.

Joseph was presumed dead, and when his brothers were sent by their aging father to buy supplies of food, Joseph took his time before disclosing who he was. First testing to see whether his father was still alive and then keeping one of them as a hostage until they returned with his younger brother, Benjamin. When finally he discloses that he is their brother Joseph, his brothers are overwhelmed with guilt, fearful of recriminations, but Joseph is full of love and compassion, and his father is overcome by joy and happiness. The whole thing is a remarkable story and well worth reading in Genesis chapters 42–46.

Ultimately, when the king hears the news, he is so pleased with Joseph that he invites the whole family to come and settle in Egypt, giving them as their abode the land at the estuary of the river, the land of Goshen (Genesis 45:16–20), where they will live for the next 430 years and multiply from 70 to something over 2,000,000 people. God had reassured Jacob that even though he was leaving Canaan, the land promised to Abraham, His promise to make them a great nation and bring them back to the land of Canaan still stood firm.

Finally, the old father Jacob dies at age 147 and, according to his dying wish, is taken back to Mamre to the land bought by Abraham and where he and his wife Sarah had been buried, to be buried in the family tomb. As an example of the esteem in which the Egyptians held Joseph, a large number of their officials travelled with the family to join in the mourning ceremony. Genesis 50:7.

Joseph himself died aged 110 years, and his body was embalmed in the Egyptian manner so that he too might be buried in the promised land.

However, things were to change for the worse, for, after Joseph's death and years after the miraculous deliverance of the nation from those 7 years of famine, we are told that a new king on the throne who had no recollection of the national debt to Joseph became alarmed at the rapid rise in numbers of this, to them, alien tribe. Fearing that they might become a political threat and potentially a military threat as well, the pharaoh ordered slave drivers to enforce hard labour on them. But despite this they still increased in number until the king issued an order that all the baby boys should be killed at birth. An order which the Hebrew midwives ignored, and so their numbers continued to rise until finally the king ordered that all the baby boys should be thrown into the river. Leaving just the girls alive. During this time, a man from the tribe of Levi married a woman from the same tribe, and first a girl was born, no problem, but some years later a baby boy was born. Unwilling to kill him, the parents, Amram and Jocabed, hid him for three months until it was no longer possible to conceal his presence. The mother hid him in a basket waterproofed with tar and hid it in the bushed at the riverbank, leaving the sister, Miriam, to watch. When Pharaoh's daughter came down to bathe, she heard a cry, discovered the child, liked what she saw, and decided to keep him as her adopted child. Miriam then sprang into action, offering to find a Hebrew woman to act as wet nurse and promptly produced her mother, who nursed him until he was old enough and then took him to Pharaoh's daughter, who adopted him, gave him the name Moses, and brought him up in the royal palace, where he was educated as a royal child and grew to be greatly respected.

Chapter 6
Moses and the Formation of a Nation

For Moses, all was apparently well for a few years, living as he did as the supposed son of Pharaoh's daughter until, aged around 40 years, he began to take a great interest in the fortunes of his own native Hebrew people and went to investigate. What he found horrified him as he saw just how badly his people were treated, and when he saw an Egyptian beat and kill one of the Hebrew slaves, when no one was looking, he went and killed the Egyptian and hid his body in the sand. The following day he went back again, but this time he saw two Hebrews fighting and challenged the one who was in the wrong. The man then turned on him, saying, "Who made you our ruler and judge?" "Are you going to kill me just as you killed that Egyptian?" Moses now realized that he had been caught out; Pharaoh, when he learned of it, tried to kill him, and now his own people were refusing to recognize his authority. His situation was perilous. Rejected by the king and without any recourse to safety with his own people, he fled and went to live in the land of Midian. Moses was a remarkable man. Brought up originally by his own parents at the command of Pharaoh's daughter, who had asked his sister, Miriam, who was watching over the cradle in the bullrushes. After he was weaned, he became the adopted son of Pharaoh's daughter, and as such, he was educated and grew up in the luxury of an Egyptian palace. However, it was his decision to identify himself with his birth relations, the Israelites, when he defended their rights by killing an oppressive Egyptian, Exodus 2:11–13, which meant that he had to make a very costly decision, Hebrews 11:24–26 a.v. Which was to give up his potentially luxurious future and, at age 40, to go out and live as a humble shepherd in the desert, with all the hardship that involved. There he met the daughters of Jethro at a well, and returning with them, even though they saw him at first as an Egyptian, he earned their trust and married Zipporah, one of the seven daughters, and stayed to act as a shepherd for his father-in-law for a further 40 years. It was this single decision which marked him out as one of God's children. One of those who, by choice but directed by God, become one of the great leaders whose lives alter the whole course of human history.

What is so significant about this is, as the Apostle Paul will later point out, Moses' transformation from being a prince of the realm of Egypt to that of a humble shepherd was a result of a conscious decision to take the side of his persecuted relatives. A decision which brought an enormous cost to him personally. A loss of wealth, of social standing, of a future as a potential king of Egypt. Most certainly there was the loss of a life of luxury and pleasure, exchanged for the role of a servant. Paul puts it more vividly. "He chose to suffer affliction with the people of God rather than enjoy the pleasures of sin for a season." Hebrews 11:25. What a price to pay, what a tremendous test, but what a more glorious future, as he was destined to deliver a nation from slavery and, having defeated the might of the Egyptian army, look after, feed, and sustain some 2,000,000 people on a forty-year journey through a desert landscape.

In the same way, the nation of Israel, despite its suffering, was to benefit enormously from having lived and worked in a nation which, as historical records show, was highly advanced technically and culturally. The Egyptian ability to build such enormous monuments, many of which are still with us, with such mathematical accuracy, and their firm commitment to an afterlife and their social and political structure would undoubtedly have given the Israelites skills and knowledge which, as pastoralists and nomads, they would have taken centuries to develop, if at all.

Moses' role as a humble shepherd was to last for forty years, almost a lifetime for most people, but it was to end most dramatically. Out one day in the Sinai desert, he came across a mysterious event. He saw a bush apparently on fire but not being consumed by the flames. Here too is a symbolical appearance of God. Symbolic because it represented the mighty power of God, as later Moses would experience at Mt. Sinai. As he drew near to investigate, he heard a voice, which told him to remove his shoes because he was in the presence of the Holy God. This unique event was even more staggering because, as far as we know and as far as is recorded, it was the first occasion for him to encounter this almighty and all-powerful God. No doubt he, like all members of Jacob's family, would have some knowledge of their ancestral God. Certainly, both his father, Amram, and his mother, Jocabed, were members of the tribe of Levi, from which the priesthood would ultimately devolve, but he had been brought up under a regime which worshipped a multitude of gods, from the sun to the river Nile and even to animal deities. On the other hand, his father-in-law, Jethro, was a priest, so although we have no record of the Israelites having any specific form of worship, the old traditions were being kept alive.

God, now speaking directly to Moses, instructs him to go back to Egypt and to deliver his now very numerous relatives from their slavery in Egypt. 'An impossible task', responds the very alarmed Moses. Impossible on several counts. There is no way that Pharaoh will agree because, in spite of their being a threat to the security of Egypt, they were an extremely valuable and free labour force at a time when, we now know, the empire was engaged in a vast building project. Great temples, enormous burial monuments, and numerous statues. All of which were labour intensive.

Further, as Moses knew, his own people had no respect for him. As when they had rejected his interference when he tried to help them when they were being beaten by their Egyptian taskmasters. Here too is a picture of the situation which Jesus would encounter when He came to save them, to deliver His people. Even more alarming for Moses was his own feeling of inadequacy and his lack of speaking ability. Then, to crown it all, he did not know which God was speaking to him, and he had to ask who this God was. "Who shall I say has told me to do this?" And the answer must have surprised him as much as it does us today, for this God simply said, "Tell them that I am the one who is eternally existing and who is not definable in human terms. I am what I will be." God is beyond human understanding. That is why later God will choose to send His own son in human likeness in order that we should be able to understand the love, the authority, and something of the power of this God. His response to the disciple Philip's question, "Show us the Father and that will satisfy us." Our Lord's reply was simply, "He that hath seen Me hath seen the Father."

However, in selecting Moses as the great leader, He had a man who, by his upbringing, had learnt a great deal about how to run a nation. In the same way, his people had acquired skills and experience which would be immeasurably useful over the coming years as God would create out of them a nation which would be even greater than the Egyptian nation. Although it would take many, many years to bring this to fruition. However, each element of this amazing event would appear to have a purpose. Moses, at first unacceptable to his own people because of his status as a prince. He would have been seen as an outsider, one who had 'chosen' to avoid the conflict of their slavery. Now, after 40 years in the very humble position of a simple shepherd, he had learned humility. To such an extent that he will rely on his older brother, Aaron, to act as his spokesman, and even his older sister, Miriam, who had been so significant in watching the baby in the rushes and had brought her mother in as a wet nurse, had been a crucial element in what was now to unfold.

There is so much more here than we are told. For example, the parents of these three children, Amram and Jocabed, were from the tribe of Levi, which would become the tribe from which the priesthood of the nation would descend. Was that family continuing the recognition of God in their lives as had the older Patriarchs, Abraham, Isaac, and Jacob, their grandfather? Indeed, as Joseph had done over 400 years earlier. Otherwise, we have no record of the 'god line' during the years of captivity, but Moses in his new state of humility was responsive when God called, which is a clear indication that he was aware of God, even if he had no personal knowledge of Him. What marked Moses out like others of the Patriarchs was this personal experience of meeting with God and entering into a unique relationship with Him. Something which was given to a very select few in the Old Testament but which, through the coming to earth of Jesus, God's Son, would become a unique experience which would mark out those who believed in Him.

It is possible to see in this remarkable event a foretelling of God's greater plan for humanity in which He would send His Son to deliver humanity from the slavery of sin and create at some point in the future a new Kingdom of God in which the true purpose of God will be unfolded. One could say of the Christian experience that God is preparing His people for a more wonderful future, that Heaven will be something which "Eye hath not seen, neither has entered into the heart of man the things which God has prepared for them that love Him." The Kingdom of God is ours. It belongs to the children of God.

Moses was to lead this great nation for 40 years. Their escape was followed by a great victory over the Egyptian army, which pursued them after their escape became known. Blocked by the Reed Sea in the Nile delta, God had opened a passage through with a great wind, enabling the whole nation to cross, only for the waters to return and drown the pursuing army. However, in spite of all the miraculous events with which God had delivered them, they never ceased to has complain. Consequently, instead of taking a quick route along the main highway into Southern Canaan, God punished them by directing them south into the Sinai

Peninsula, where they suffered great privation and experienced God's power in delivering them until all of the adults who had left Egypt had died. What the Bible record does not tell is how they spent those years. Thirty-eight years passed from leaving Kadesh Barnea before they finally entered the land at Jericho. Clearly, a vast number of people now. They had 600,000 men armed for battle, which implies a total number in excess of 2,000,000, and they had very extensive flocks and herds. Obviously, they would have encamped for prolonged periods. Long enough to plant and reap a harvest, staying until the pasturage was exhausted, then moving on to another fertile area. Frequently short of water and supplies, they were fed and given water at times by the miraculous provision of God. Water from the rock and manna from heaven. Even a flock of quails when they demanded meat. Then, before they were prepared to attempt the invasion of their promised land, they sent out spies to survey the land. Spies who came back laden with produce, enormous bunches of grapes, but also with news of fortified cities populated by giants, and of the twelve men sent, only two recommended that with God's help they could win through. Those two were Joshua and Caleb. Even Miriam and Aaron died on the journey. Both of them had failed. Both had suffered from jealousy of Moses, criticizing him, which resulted in Miriam being smitten with leprosy and only healed when her brother, Moses, prayed for her. Aaron too had failed. Whilst Moses was on Mt. Sinai receiving the Laws, because he was away for some forty days, Aaron had responded to the demand by the people to create a god of their own making, whom they could worship. Moses too had failed to give the honour to God when he struck the rock to produce water at Rephidim. Aged 120 years, he was given a glimpse of the promised land, but even he was not allowed to enter the land.

So, we find in Moses a great leader whose greatness derived from two things. A personal experience of God and a willingness to deny the prospect of wealth and prestige to accept the humility of a life as a shepherd. When he did that, he was then a suitable candidate for the much greater role as the leader of a nation that was to become God's chosen race. But even he was not perfect; acting when told to draw water from the rock to provide for the multitude of the people, by striking the rock as he did, he failed to give the credit, the honour, to God. Which act was to become again symbolic, referring as it did to the suffering which God's Son Jesus would later suffer at the hands of His own people.

However, great though Moses was as a leader, his greatest and most important contribution to the service of God was in his introduction of the Law, which he received personally from God on Mt. Sinai, and the consequent erection of the Tabernacle, the Tent of God's presence, and the establishing of the Priesthood and all the functions of their worship, which would have a profound effect on the nation and which are still recognized by orthodox Jews in this twenty-first century.

And the reason behind this is what Paul explains to the Jews in Rome, writing in his Epistle to the Romans, chapters 7 and 8. What he explains is that until the Law was given there was no real awareness of sin. Until they were strictly told not to commit adultery, not to steal, not to bear false witness, and to only worship Jehovah, their God, there was no understanding that these things were wrong. To steal or to commit adultery might annoy or upset one's neighbour and indeed cause suffering, but the law defined these as 'sinful' as acts against God, and the law provided the prescribed punishment. However, as Paul points out, the Law could define sin, but it could not stop people from obeying natural instincts. Human nature is, in the first place, selfish. It acts in accordance with desire, and because human nature is weak, it drives people to satisfy those desires. And this is why the law was weak, because it depended on human nature, and human nature was weak. Romans 8:3 "What the law could not do because human nature was weak, God did. He condemned sin in human nature by sending His own Son, who came with a nature like sinful human nature, to do away with sin."

The effect of these 'reforms' was to introduce moral responsibility to the nation, and from here on in the life of the nation, people and nations would be judged, not by human standards, but by God's standards.

Joshua

We first meet Joshua as a young man described as Moses' helper. His original name was Hoshea, the son of Nun, but he was renamed Joshua by Moses when he was selected as one of the 12 spies sent to reconnoitre the land as they camped ready to enter. He and Caleb confirmed that with God's presence and blessing they could overcome all opponents and occupy this very fertile land. The other ten spies reported that there were giants in the land and the territory was not worth the cost of capturing it. There is no dramatic encounter with God and no suggestion of the very important role which will bring him to prominence as the leader chosen to follow Moses and to take the Israelites into the Promised Land. Yet ultimately, he will have a whole book of the Bible named after him. He is first named in Exodus 17 when Moses sends him to defeat an attack of the

Amalekites following a very sad time when the Israelites, having been camped at Rephidim, complained about a lack of water and told Moses that it was all his fault for bringing them out of Egypt, where they had food and water, only for them to die of thirst in the desert. In response, God provides water from the rock, but Moses also angers God by behaving badly when performing the miracle. An act which would cost him dearly as God refused to allow him into the Promised Land. However, Joshua was successful in the battle against Amalek because Moses intervened with God. Holding up his arms in prayer. Exodus 17:12. God told them to record this victory, telling Joshua that he would fight for them against that same enemy in the future.

We next meet him when Moses is called to go up Mt. Sinai to receive the stone tablets containing all the laws for the instruction of the people, and we are told in Exodus 24:13 that Moses and his helper, Joshua, got ready to ascend the mountain. Though we are not told if he actually went up to the presence of God. But it is likely that he did, for on the way down, Exodus 32:17, it was Joshua who heard the people shouting. They had commanded Aaron to make a golden calf, which they had dedicated as a god, the god whom they said had brought them out of Egypt. This disastrous event would give rise to God saying later that they had never worshipped Him in sincerity.

A further indication of Joshua's role comes in Exodus 33:11; we are told that on occasion when Moses entered the Tent of the Presence to meet God, Moses would then leave the Tent, but Joshua, the young man who was his helper, stayed in the Tent. Indicating that Joshua was being prepared for a leading role, as one who was able to enter the presence of God.

Later we find him chosen as one of the twelve spies send to survey the land of Canaan (Numbers 13:16), and finally he is appointed as Moses' successor (Numbers 27:12–18). The rest of his life and his exploits are recorded in the book of Joshua and detail his miraculous crossing of the river Jordan, the capture of the city of Jericho and then the division of the land between the twelve tribes of Israel, 14–21. This included the permission for Reuben, Gad, and half the tribe of Manasseh to populate the land east of the Jordan on the condition that they fought with the other tribes during the conquest before finally, when the land was subdued, they returned home. In chapter 24, we read of his death at the age of 110 years after having made the Israelites renew their vow of loyalty and to keep the Covenant with their God. What this record does not tell is the number of battles which he fought against some very formidable enemies. Perhaps the greatest of these was against the fortified city of Hazor, which he captured and burnt. The archaeological evidence of which is still there, and the city lay waste for many years until it was rebuilt, probably by King Solomon, as a defence of his Northern frontier and as a place where he maintained an army garrison. There is no question that as a leader, Joshua was a man approved of by God, and it was through his inspired leadership that the nation was able to force an entry against the resident nations. His ability being reflected in the succeeding years when the decline set in after his death, and the nation failed to complete the conquest, with the result that as a disunited, tribal force, they came under attack from the local nations who clearly resented any attempt to seize land and property. In fact, it was not until David became king that the nation was able to establish its complete hold over the land, and he spent most of his life doing that, paving the way for the nation to achieve the highest status under his son Solomon.

Altogether a remarkable life for Joshua, the son of Nun. His value only being fully recognized after his death, as we shall see. But before we leave him, we need to consider a number of things. Joshua died at age 110. If he began to work with Moses at the age of, say, 15, add the 40 years of the journey from Egypt, then he would have been some 55 years of age when they entered the land of Canaan and a further 55 years before the initial conquest was over. At this point the soldiers from Reuben, Gad, and half Manasseh went home to their own lands on the east of the river Jordan, leaving nine and a half tribes on the western side of the river, and presumably the army was stood down as a combined national force. Now each of the very scattered tribes would be attempting to secure their own areas of land from the enemies which surrounded them. Most notably the Philistines in the South, who would trouble Israel for centuries, right through the period of the Judges and into the reign of both Saul and David, and the tribes like the Midianites and then the Sidonians and the Hivites in the North. In fact, what we must recognise is that without one unifying leader, the individual tribes were relatively weak. A situation which was made worse by their idolatry, which alienated them from their unique source of strength, their God, Jehovah. See also Judges 2:6; the nation remained strong during Joshua's life, but after his death they, once again, forgot how and why they were there. Joshua 24:31.

Chapter 7
The Interim Period of
The Judges as Tribal Leaders

Originally judges had been appointed by Moses on the advice of his father-in-law Jethro, the priest of Midian (Exodus 18:13–26). As helpers under the guidance of Moses, they were invaluable and greatly reduced the pressure on Moses, as indeed Jethro had told him. However, after the death of Joshua and at the Lord's direction, two tribes, Judah and Benjamin, set out to attack the Canaanites and were successful in capturing a number of cities. They were followed in their military success by the tribes of Ephraim and Manasseh. But they failed in that although they secured some victories, they did not drive out their enemies (Judges 1:27), and that was followed by a list of other tribes who disobeyed the direct command of God, which was to drive their enemies out. This failure prompted a strong rebuke from God, Judges 2:1, in which He reminded them that His Covenant with Israel required their total compliance to destroy these pagan tribes and the worship of their gods. And this meant not making any () covenant with the local people and tearing () down and destroying their heathen altars. God also said that because of their rank disobedience, in which they had failed to wipe out these false and man-made gods and by compromising with them had done the opposite. Therefore, He would NOT drive out their enemies before them, and furthermore, they would in turn become trapped by the worship of the pagan gods. Judges 2:3.

This was catastrophic. Whilst Joshua and the other leaders had been alive, they and their predecessors, men who had experienced the mighty power of God, had faithfully served the Lord. But, after the death of the previous generation, Judges 2:11, they had effectively stopped worshipping the Lord, the God of their ancestors, the God who had brought them out of Egypt so powerfully and miraculously and had begun to worship the pagan gods of the very nations they had been told to destroy. Getting rid of pagan worship had been one of the main intentions of their conquest of the land.

Consequently, God was absolutely furious with them (2:14) and allowed their enemies to attack and overpower them. This then is the background to this next phase of the nation's existence. However, there was a purpose behind this, as the scripture narrative points out, Judges 3:1. "The Lord left some nations in the land to test the Israelites who had not been through the wars in Canaan." And verse 4, "They were to be a test for Israel, to find out whether or not the Israelites would obey the commands which the Lord had given to their ancestors through Moses." Which indicated that God was using even their failures to further His purposes. The issue is summed up in Joshua 24:31 and repeated in Judges 2:6. "As long as Joshua was alive, the people served the Lord, and after his death, they continued to do so so long as the leaders were alive who had seen for themselves all the great things the Lord had done for Israel." Verse 10 then states, "That whole generation also died, and the next generation forgot the Lord and what He had done for Israel."

Compromise is always a problem, most especially when it weakens the uniqueness of a community, but equally so when individuals compromise their principles for the sake of progress or material success or even to secure peace. For the Christian, life can become a spiritual battle between the natural demands of the flesh, pride and ambition, and the claim of God, which requires total commitment. Just as Jesus had to be prepared to sacrifice his life and dedicate His whole existence, in order to fulfil God's purpose through Him.

Following the death of Joshua, we have a period of some 150 years of deep trouble for the nation, in which they would then cry to God for help and He would then send a succession of leaders to rescue them before the institution of the role of kings, which would, under King David, reunite these disparate tribes once again. In this interim period of testing, a time, we must remember, when the twelve tribes were widely scattered over a very large territory, God rescued His people by choosing a number of local men and women. Tribal leaders, if you like, to rescue them. Part of the problem was the very nature of the territory of this land of Canaan, which comprised a series of hills and valleys. In which local tribes and groups had, over the years, established themselves and against which the Israelites had to compete as they sought to claim farmland and pasture for their extensive flocks and herds. Possession of land was vital for their future.

What we must understand is that the whole of that mountainous and fertile region was ruled by 'petty kings', prima facie rulers of a group of cities, rather than being like the major nations surrounding them, such as Egypt and, in Mesopotamia, the Hittites, who were long-time enemies of Egypt. All of these 'petty kings' were contending for control of land, both to provide pastorage for their animals and to cultivate. Whilst the wider peripheral surrounding area came under the authority of the Syrians and the Assyrians, who represented a far more formidable threat to the whole area.

At this time the Israelites were a widely scattered group comprising twelve separate tribes, each under its own leader. After the death of Joshua, the whole nation lacked cohesion. Loyalty to their father, Jacob, and even more, to their founding father Abraham's principles of loyalty to God and His Covenant. These things became less important to them than the acquisition of pasturage and localized defensive positions. Their problems arose because they had failed to drive out the pagan tribes, who then attacked the Israelites and robbed them. But even more destructive was the fact that they intermarried with their enemies and adopted the worship of their pagan gods. Both things strictly forbidden by God. In doing so they lost their unique heritage and their remarkable relationship with God. "Come ye out from among them and be ye separate, saith the Lord." 2 Corinthians 6:17 AV.

This situation is well illustrated by our own situation here in England after the Romans left, when, because there was no acceptable unifying authority, the various regions not only contended against each other but were vulnerable to attack. It was not until the Norman conquest that rulers were able to unite the country. Harold Godwinson, the Saxon King, had failed to do this, enabling his cousin, William Duke of Normandy, to replace him and, by force of arms, exercise control. Even then, as history shows, there were divisions between local landowners and the king which even Magna Carta in the 12th century did not resolve, and although the conflict at that time was between local barons and the King, the right to justice independent of the King was not finally resolved until the authority of Parliament was established, which effectively reduced the authority of the king, largely by exercising the right of Parliament alone to raise taxes but also by establishing the right of every citizen to be judged by a panel of his peers, not by the king.

In Israel, however, amongst these leaders, some individuals achieved considerable fame and were regarded as heroes by their contemporaries. In the case of this God-led and inspired nation, invariably these leaders were chosen by God and equipped and enabled by Him with the double purpose both of preserving the integrity of the nation and reminding them that their very existence was at all times dependent upon their father, God. Disobedience, disloyalty, and failure to conform to the Covenant established in the time of Moses would incur the wrath of God, as clearly stated in the Covenant, which, in effect, was conditional upon the compliance of the recipients.

What we are about to see during this period is the evidence of a problem of leadership which will plague this nation and indeed would be problematic for all nations, as with the Greeks from the time of Socrates. The early Hebraic leaders were the authority both in the political and social sense as well as being responsible for the nation's spiritual well-being. Combined in one person, those two responsibilities had become too much for one man. Which is why Moses' father-in-law, Jethro, had advocated the appointing of judges. And the New Testament, in the same way, the new Church appointed deacons to administer the social aspects of their society. Acts chapter 6.

The first of these military leaders was Othniel, whom God chose to help them at a time when the king of Mesopotamia had conquered them and, for a period of eight years, kept them in his power. Then the Lord responded to their cries and sent to help them Othniel, who was the son of Caleb's younger brother. As a demonstration both of His power and His love for the nation, God then gave Othniel a great victory over the king of Mesopotamia. Victory to such an extent that Israel enjoyed peace for some forty years as news of the nation's military success percolated through to other neighbouring nations.

However, after his death, the people, who appeared to have learned nothing from their previous experience and with a new younger generation growing up, once again forsook the worship of their God, by whose actions on their behalf they had been delivered from years of abject slavery in Egypt. As a result, to bring them to their senses, God allowed a joint force, comprised of men of Moab, Ammon, and Amalek under the leadership of King Eglon of Moab, to invade and capture the key city of Jericho and thereby to control the nation for some eighteen years until, in their distress, they came to their senses and cried out to their powerful God for help, once again.

This time God chose a man named Ehud, a left-handed warrior from the tribe of Benjamin. He played a deadly trick on the king. Having been sent by the nation with gifts to negotiate with the king, he had made himself a double-edged sword, which he wore on his right side. Having presented the gifts, he sent his colleagues away and he himself left only to return shortly after with a message for the king. At which the king sent his servants away, seeing no threat in a sword on the wrong side. Then, saying that he had a message from God for him, he drew his sword with his left hand and thrust it into the stomach of the king, who was grossly fat. So fat, in fact, that the sword came out at his back and the fat covered the handle. Ehud then closed the door of the room, locked it, and left. His servants thought he was relieving himself and left the king undisturbed whilst Ehud escaped.

Having escaped and having killed their opponent, Ehud then summoned the soldiers of Israel, pursued the Moabite army, and by preventing them from escaping over the Jordan, slaughtered some 10,000 of them and put an end to their oppression of the nation, giving them peace for 80 years. In other words, when God intervened in behalf of Israel, He gave them a conclusive victory, which was only ended when the nation once again forgot their need of God's help and became irresponsibly sinful. Either because they did not recognize the importance of God's presence with them or because they preferred the pleasures of sin.

God finally came to their rescue again, obviously because He wanted to preserve the nation for a future purpose, not because they repented and altered their ways. This time their heroic deliverer was a man named Shamgar, who delivered Israel from their enemies on the western side by killing 600 Philistines with an ox goad. Remember that when Israel was living under the authority of an enemy, the usual practice was to deny their army access to any weapons. Even their farming tools would have to be taken to an authorised farrier to be sharpened.

The next sequence of events was that God allowed the nation to be conquered by King Jabin, a Canaanite king who ruled from the very heavily fortified city of Hazor in the north and whose army was led by a warrior named Sisera. This Sisera had a strong force under him, which included 900 iron chariots, a very formidable force rather equivalent to our modern tanks. At this period the Israelites were simply foot soldiers. Whereas the enemies chariots were fast, manoeuvrable, and often had two occupants. One to drive and the other to fire arrows. They could sweep down very rapidly and, made of iron, were able to withstand a lot of enemy fire. This went on for some twenty years, and once again, in their desperation, the people cried to God for help. But this time help was to come from a woman. Deborah. Deborah, herself a married woman, was acting as a judge at the time, operating from a situation between Bethel and Ramah, and people would go to her for decisions. On one occasion she sent a message to a man named Barak, the son of Abinoam telling him that God had told him to take 10,000 men from the tribes of Naphtali and Zebulun, to go to Mt Tabor where he would bring Sisera and Jabin's army to fight against him at the river Kishon. God also said that even though Sisera would bring an army and his feared iron chariots, He would give him victory.

Unfortunately, Barak was afraid that God would not do what He said, so he told Deborah that he would only go to the battle if she went with him. She agreed but warned him that he would get no credit for the victory because God would hand Sisera over to a woman. So, they went off together.

In the meantime, Heber the Kenite, one of the descendants of Moses' brother-in-law, was living nearby, and he and his family were at peace with Jabin. Then, when Barak, at Deborah's command, led his forces down the hill to attack Sisera's force, God caused Sisera's men to panic. Barak pursued them and killed the whole lot, except for Sisera, who ran away. He saw the tent of Jael, Heber's wife, and went in to hide. Jael gave him a drink of milk, and he, tired out, fell fast asleep. Jael then picked up a hammer and a tent peg and drove it through his skull. Later, when Barak came looking for Sisera, Jael came out, called him and showed him his enemy, dead.

Following that signal victory, the Israelites continued to attack Hazor until they finally destroyed it, and the nation enjoyed peace for 40 years.

Gideon

Israel was in trouble again, this time from the Midianites and the Amalekites, who used to come and raid the farms at harvest time to steal the produce. Their raiding bands were so fierce, and Israel, without an army or any coordinated response, was at their mercy. So much so that they hid themselves in caves and in the hills. Judges chapter 6. This situation went on for quite a period of time, some seven years, during which time the raiders would come with their livestock and camels and devastate the area until at last the people cried out to their God for help, and He sent them yet another prophet who simply and bluntly told them the truth. They had neglected the worship of their true God and had adopted the worship of the Amorites, amongst whom they were living. As a result, as they had repeatedly been warned, God had allowed them to suffer from the hands of those very people whose worship they had favoured.

At last God relented and sent an angel messenger who came and sat under an oak tree belonging to Joash from the tribe of Abiezer, whose son Gideon was evading the depravations of the Midianites by threshing his wheat in a wine press.

Obviously, Gideon stood out as a man who was intelligent and capable, but even he was mortally afraid of the Midianite invaders and powerless to help his tribe or his nation. However, when the angel appeared, he addressed Gideon with the words, "The Lord is with you, brave and mighty man." To which Gideon replied, "If the Lord is with us, why has all this happened? What about all the wonderful things that our fathers told us the Lord used to do – how He brought them out of Egypt? The lord has abandoned us and left us to the mercy of the Midianites."

God was able to respond to that challenge, for here was a man who recognised how effective the power of God had been in the past, a man who realised that the nation's success in the past had been down to the power of God, not to the might of their armies. Here was the reality of the situation which the nation as a whole was unwilling to accept. They had to realise that by abandoning God, they were left to rely on their own resources, which were not equal to the task, and it was only when they realised that fact, as Gideon was doing here, that God could step in and help, and this fact had to be made clear to them, as we shall see.

The Lord then ordered Gideon, "Go with all your strength and rescue Israel from the Midianites. I Myself am sending you." Judges 6:14.

Now, just as happened with Moses all those years ago, come the excuses. I am the weakest man in a small and weak tribe, the least important member of my family. Good! For the message of the Gospel is that God's strength is made perfect in our weakness, that the power might be seen to be of God and not of man. 2 Corinthians 12:9. And what God will now do through Gideon is designed to demonstrate just that. God tells him that he can defeat the Midianites because He, Almighty God, will be with him, and he will crush the Midianites as if they were one man. However, faced with what appears to be an impossible task, Gideon wants to see some evidence that it is God, the God of their fathers, who is speaking to him. And the proof? Gideon offered a food offering and asked the 'angel' to wait whilst he went off and prepared and cooked a meal. Then when he returned with the food, he was told to put the meat and the bread on top of a rock and pour the broth over them. Then the angel reached out with the stick which was in his hand and touched the meat and the bread, and fire came out of the rock and burnt up the bread and the meat. Then the angel disappeared.

Staggered by all this, he cried out in fear and absolute terror, "Sovereign Lord! I have seen your angel face face-to-face." But the response from heaven was simply, "Peace Don't be afraid. You will not die." And Gideon built an altar there and named it. "The Lord is peace." Judges 6:22.

But Gideon's testing was not over, for the task was immense, and Gideon still needed to demonstrate the extent of his ability to obey. To carry out orders implicitly. So God now told him to put his life on the line. He had to destroy his father's altar to Baal, cut down the image dedicated to the goddess Asherah, build a well-constructed altar to the Lord, and then offer on it a sacrifice comprised of his father's bull and a second bull and burn them on the altar to God. Which was a dramatic and personal statement which would, by destroying the local deity and imposing the worship of the God of Abraham and Isaac, make a public statement but at the risk of his own life. Effectively he was offering his own personal safety, and he was so afraid of his family and the reaction of the town that he took ten of his servants, and they did it at night.

However, as yet another demonstration that God was with him, in the morning his father stood by him and faced the angry mob with the words, "Are you defending Baal? Anyone who stands up for him will be killed before morning. If Baal is a god, let him defend himself."

But Gideon's actions alerted the Amalekites and the Midianites, who gathered their forces and came out for battle. Gideon, at the prompting of the Holy Spirit, called out all the neighbouring Israelite tribes, Manasseh, Asher, Zebulun, and Naphtali, who did come to join him. So now he had an army which numbered over 30,000 men, but still he was unsure and asked God for further proof. This time he asked God that a fleece left out overnight would be wet, but the ground dry. And the following night he reversed it, fleece dry and ground wet, and God did that very thing for him.

But still, this was not enough to demonstrate where the victory was coming from, so Gideon was told to tell his men that any who were afraid should go home and not weaken the resolve of the army. 22,000 went home, leaving just 10,000 soldiers. But these were too many, so God devised another method to reduce the numbers by getting the men to drink from a stream and selecting only those, 300 in number, who scooped up the water in their hands to drink instead of kneeling down and lapping like a dog. The reason: "The men you have are too many for Me to give them victory over the Midianites. They might think that they had won by themselves and so give Me no credit." Judges 7:2

However, Gideon was now even more afraid, so one more thing to encourage him. "If you are afraid," said God, "take your servant and go down into the camp and listen to what they are saying." And what heard was one soldier recounting to another a dream in which a loaf of bread rolled into their camp and hit a tent, which collapsed. To which his colleague responded, "It is the sword of Gideon; it can't mean anything else." "God has given him victory over Midian and our whole army."

Gideon then divided his men into three groups, each one hundred strong, armed with lamps hidden in a pitcher held in one hand and a trumpet in the other. Just before midnight at a signal. The men smashed their pitchers, letting the light shine out, blew their trumpets, and shouted, "A sword for the Lord and for Gideon." At which the whole camp was thrown into a panic and the men ran away yelling, and while the trumpets were sounding, the Lord made the enemy attack each other in the confusion, whilst at that point the Israelite army was called out to pursue the fleeing men, cutting them off at the Jordan River crossing. Of the combined army of some 120,000 soldiers, only about 15,000 were left, and Gideon continued pursuing them and captured the two Midianite kings, Zebah and Zalmunna, which caused the whole army to panic.

The only sad thing was the failure of the men of Sukkoth to aid the army when, exhausted and hungry, they crossed the Jordan, and they were severely punished on Gideon's return. The men of Ephraim were also angry that Gideon had not called them out, but in fact their defeat of two other of the leaders, Oreb and Zeeb, meant that they had made a valuable contribution to the defeat of Midian, so they were mollified.

There were no doubt many other tribal leaders who exercised bravery during these 150 years of disorganized warfare, and we shall look at some more, but the account of Gideon's remarkable victory is a lesson to all, in his day and ours, of the way in which when God finds men and women of faith, He can act miraculously in a manner which will bring glory to His name and declare His power to others. Gideon's victory was so complete that the nation had peace for 40 years, until his death, when once again they reverted to the worship of the Baals; they were not even thankful for all the good which Gideon had done.

God's servant was forgotten along with the God whom he had so faithfully served. Two of his sons tried to follow, but they were divisive figures only caused more confusion.

Jephthah

The next figure of any note was a man named Jephthah. For some eighteen years the tribes east of the Jordan had persecuted the Israelites of Reuben, Gad, and Manasseh who had settled there, and then they grew bolder and crossed the river to attack Judah, Ephraim, and Benjamin as well. This meant that the Southern part of the country was in turmoil, and once again, in deep distress, they cried out to the Lord to rescue them. Their old history was being repeated because they refused to learn from the mistakes of the past, and God reminded them of just that. Again and again God had delivered the nation. From the Egyptians, the Amorites, the Ammonites, the Philistines, the Amalekites, and the Sidonians, but after every intervention by God, they had returned to idolatry, to the worship of the very gods they had been told to drive out and to utterly destroy. To destroy them because they were opposed to God. They were gods who were worshipped by the practice of obscenities, who encouraged practices which refuted the holiness and loving kindness of God, and claimed as their possession the things which God had created. Making human vanities and human proclivities the object of human desires and glorifying human weakness.

However, Israel was now so desperate that they simply said, "We have sinned. Do what you like, but please save us today." Further, they did actually give up many of their idolatrous practices and turned back to the Lord until He recognized their distress and prepared to help them. They in turn looked for a leader, and they picked on a most unlikely candidate, Jephthah, a very courageous and resourceful soldier but one who was an outcast from their society. Jephthah was the son of Gilead, a tribal leader, but he was illegitimate and had been rejected by his family. Now they turned to him, and he, seeing an opportunity for advancement, agreed to lead them on the condition that if he was victorious, he would become their leader (Judges 11:9).

Jephthah's political ability and intelligence were shown in the way in which he approached the task. He went first to the leader of the Ammonites to ask why they were amassing their forces in such an aggressive manner. The king replied, "When the Israelites came out from Egypt, they took away my land from the

River Arnon to the River Jabbok and the River Jordan. Now you must give it back peacefully."

Jephthah corrected him, reminding him that when Israel requested permission to cross their land, their king refused, forcing Israel to make a huge detour in order to arrive at the other side of the River Arnon to the East. When they arrived there, they asked permission from the Amorite king Sihon, but he too refused and gathered a great army to oppose them, but the Lord gave them victory over Sihon, and they occupied all his land. "Now." Said Jephthah, "Are you trying to take it back? You can keep what your god Chemosh has given you, but we are going to keep everything that the Lord our God has given us." He further added that they were in the wrong by making war against Israel and that the Lord would be the judge. The king of Ammon ignored him.

By making this a religious issue in defence of their God, the Lord Himself honoured Jephthah, and the Spirit of the Lord came on him. Like Gideon before him, this man, despite his unfavourable background, was in turn a man whom God could use because he acknowledged God as the true source of his strength. He did not rely on his own qualities but freely acknowledged the power of God. He even went as far as vowing to the Lord that if God gave him victory, he would sacrifice to God the first person from his house to greet him on his return. The result was a glorious and complete rout of the Ammonite army. Sadly, however, it was his daughter, his only child, who came out to greet him, singing and dancing. And she, as well as her father, paid the price.

Men like Gideon and Jephthah were seen as heroic role models because they acknowledged that their victories were a demonstration of the power of God, not dependent on human resources but which demonstrated the power and the glory of God. Important because each of these events, as with Moses' remarkable career, were pointing forward to the work of Christ and His Apostles, each of whom paid an enormous price to fulfil the purpose of God for humanity and indeed for Creation. A creation formed by God through Jesus Christ, Hebrews 1:2. A creation doomed by the waywardness of humanity and which took the sacrifice of His Son Jesus to redeem. A creation which is being recreated by Jesus, Romans 8:19–21 with a new creation which begins in humanity with what Jesus described to Nicodemus as a 'new birth' John 3:6.

Samson

The next and indeed the last of these great figures who feature in that turbulent 150 years from the death of Joshua to the first of the kings was Samson, a very different figure from his predecessors. Samuel was a man marked from birth at a time when Israel had been suffering from the depredations of the Philistines for some 40 years. His parents from the tribe of Dan had been childless when an angel of the Lord appeared to Manoah's wife to tell her that she would have a son but that he should be dedicated to the Lord as a Nazirite. This required that he avoid alcohol and that from birth his hair must not be cut. Manoah's wife told her husband that a man of God had visited her, a man who looked as frightening as an angel. Manoah then asked the Lord to send the man back to tell them what they should do with the boy when he was born.

The angel reappeared to the woman as she sat in the fields, and she ran to call her husband, who asked the man for further instructions, which were that his wife should also live in accordance with the Nazirite vow during her pregnancy and that the child should also be brought up in accordance with that vow. Not realizing that it was an angel, Manoah offered the man hospitality, which he refused, saying, "If you want to prepare food, burn it as an offering to the Lord."

Manoah then asked the man his name and was told that it was "a name of wonder." Then when Manoah offered the meal as a sacrifice, they saw the Lord's angel go up towards heaven in the flames, and they realised then that it had been an angel of the Lord. They were both now afraid that they would die, but the wife, very wisely, said that if God wanted to kill them, he would not have either accepted their offering or told them such important things. Clearly, she too was a woman of faith in the actions of their God.

In due course the woman gave birth to a son and named him Samson and brought him up in the strict codes of the Nazarites, which, amongst other things, meant that he never cut his hair or drank any alcohol. His long hair was a symbol of his total dedication to the service of God. However, as he grew to manhood, he began to give evidence of unusual physical strength. The Bible records a number of these unusually large men who dominated their surroundings. Men such as Goliath, who challenged the whole Israelite army, only to be slain by a young shepherd lad named David using only a sling and a stone but who came in the name of the Lord.

The most notable factor in the life of Samson was that God used his unique strength to unsettle Israel's long-time enemies, the Philistines, and He did it by means of his unique relationship with God. He became an absolute terror to the Philistine nation. However, he fell in love with a Philistine girl, Delilah, who was used by her own people to find out what gave him his unique strength and forced her to betray him by threatening her and her family. A classic case of a man being deceived by his love for a woman.

Sadly, the result was that Samson surrendered the secret of his strength, which was his vow as a Nazarite, the symbol of which was his hair, which had not been cut since his birth. But the loss of his hair was also symbolic of his failure to live a godly life, and as a result, he was captured by his great enemies, the Philistines. However, as his hair grew again in captivity, God gave him one last chance to prove himself the champion of God. The Philistines were holding a great celebration of their victory by offering a sacrifice to the god Dagon, and they sent for the blind Samson to make fun of him, to humiliate him, and to demonstrate that their god Dagon was greater than the God of the Israelites.

Standing between two of the great pillars which supported the roof and seizing the opportunity, his hair having grown, Samson cried one last time to God for His help and then, seizing two of the pillars which supported the roof of the great chamber, he prayed. "Sovereign Lord…remember me, please. God, give me my strength once more so that with this blow I can get even with the Philistines for putting out my two eyes." He then pushed against the two pillars with all his strength, and the whole building collapsed, killing more of his enemies with that one act than he had in all his previous life. This story in its full splendour is detailed in John Milton's great epic poem, "Samson Agonistes." Which he wrote in the years immediately after he became totally blind, and it was a kind of tour de force to demonstrate that God was still with him despite his handicap.

Following the death of Samson, the nation was again at the mercy of its enemies, although we are given the account of some further heroic characters who helped to maintain their contact with their God until we reach a major turning point with the birth of a most remarkable figure at a time when the old established priesthood under Eli was falling apart because of the dissolute behaviour of his two sons, Hophni and Phinehas.

We are left with the question, "Why did God select these individuals to serve Him?" They were ordinary people, often of little consequence in their own society. And yet, that was most probably the reason why they were chosen. Paul explains this in his letter to the Ephesians, 2:. "Not of works (human effort) lest any man should boast." That is why Gideon was told to reduce his army to fight the Midianites from 32,000 men to just 300. Judge 7: 2–7 av. The nation had to understand that it was God who was delivering them, not their own efforts, however valiant and courageous they might have been.

Samuel The Prophet

During the period of the Judges, the spiritual welfare of the nation had been in the hands of the priests, the last of whom, Eli, was now an old man whose sons, Hophni and Phinehas, were profligate rascals who used their position to live sensorially and above authority. However now, Eli the Priest would be succeeded by a young child who had been placed in his care and under his authority by his mother.

This child was one of the most outstanding, charismatic figures of the Old Testament. Named Samue by his mother, who had dedicated him to the Lord from his birth, he would be called a prophet, and as such he would exercise a key role in the future of this nation. As a prophet he would act as an intermediary between God and man. As one of the last of the then 'so-called' judges, his role would be in administration and the execution of justice and the law so that his word would have been accepted as final in legal and religious matters. But it is in his role as a unique intermediary between the nation and God that his greatest work lies.

This was a period in the history of the nation when 'church and state' were a combined office because the ultimate purpose for these people was seen to be to please God. This issue of the relationship between religious leaders and state administrators has arisen a number of times over the succeeding centuries, and, today, it is still an issue of debate. One of our recent prelates at the head of the Church in England, William Temple, warned of the problems which arise in modern times if the two are combined.

For many centuries the Roman Catholic Church sought to exercise authority, both temporal and religious, over the world's rulers, claiming that authority from the legacy of Peter, but it originates really in the so-called conversion of the Roman Emperor Constantine in the 4th century. He had claimed that his recent victory at Milvain Bridge had come after he saw a vision of the Cross of Christ in the sky. However, politically he was canny enough to see that the Christian Church of his day was expanding rapidly and that the new converts were amenable to the disciple that the church imposed, just at a time when Roman influence throughout their empire was declining. However, this did not prevent the decline and fall of that Roman empire in the 5th century, whereas the Church continued to thrive and prosper`.

One of the major acts of Constantine at the conference of bishops, which he called at Nicaea in 312, was to establish the world-wide authority of the Church through its bishops. After his death the Church, in Rome, assumed the right to continue its authority as leader of the Christian world with the Pope being regarded as Peter's successor. This led to some ten centuries in which the Church sought to control the political activities of the world. Which they did by claiming to have the right to grant access to heaven only to those who observed its sacraments. To be excommunicated by the Church was to mean that one's soul would end either in Hell or, at best, in Purgatory. The only way out from that was to pay the Church to perform 'masses' on behalf of the victim. To forgive sin on payment of money. It was not until the 16th century that the monk Martin Luther challenged this and reintroduced the idea of salvation by faith in the finished work of Christ on the Cross. Luther maintained that mankind could only find salvation through the grace of God and the sacrifice of His Son on the Cross. Which was an unmerited act of God's love and not by any work or payment we could make to the church.

In fact, the right of the Pope to have political as well as religious authority continued for many centuries until it was challenged by the reformers, such as Martin Luther, a priest in the church who, in 1514, challenged the authority of the church and the Pope to grant 'indulgences', automatic forgiveness of sin, an 'indulgence', as it was called, on payment of money. In his thesis for a debate of 39 articles, he challenged the church of which he was a part, and it was he who, aided later by some nations, rebutted this Papal authority. As happened in England under Henry VIII. Ironically, this was the result of Henry's desire to have a male heir by divorcing his wife, Catherine of Aragon, who had been unable to provide a male heir, her only living child being Mary. The divorce was rejected by the Pope so, at the advice of his counsellors who, undoubtedly, were angry that an absent ruler should have any authority over the affairs of the kingdom, Henry personally took control of the Church in England and was then able to have the marriage annulled. Thereby forming what has subsequently been known as the Church of England. But this was not a singular event because the 'Protestant' reformers were gathering strength, aided by the new translations of the Bible, which were replacing the old Latin Vulgate of Jerome. This in turn was aided by the discovery of 'printing' by Gutenberg in Germany, which enabled the new translations to be printed and copied rapidly and inexpensively compared with the old handwritten versions produced by monks in the monasteries.

However, the issue of the relationship between church and state has been a thorny one for centuries. From the concept of the 'divine right of kings' under which kings took their authority from God and not their public, an idea echoed in the act whereby our kings and queens are anointed with oil at their coronation. To the concept that Divine law is also civil law, as in many Muslim nations today, to the disestablishment of the church, which separates the religious leaders from civil authority, even when there is a 'state church', as is basically the situation in the UK, even though bishops of the church have a seat in the House of Lords. In the US there is no state church, but under their constitution everyone has the right to worship whom and as they please. Italy and Spain are Catholic countries, but the church has no say in government; in fact, in Italy the Vatican is a separate state in its own right. The MAGA movement in America now is trying to push for a return to the religious ideals of the Founding Fathers. However, as Archbishop William Temple points out in his book on Christianity and the State (Macmillan 1925), politics and religion have different and conflicting goals for the people whom they represent.

However, as we return to the life of Samuel, we see how progressively the roles of national or political leader and that of religious leaders would become separated after Samuel's death.

Samuel is one of the finest examples of what is meant by 'the children of God'. From before his birth, he was marked out as different. His mother, Hannah, had been childless and, as such, had been mocked by her companion wife and had become desperate, feeling that without a child her life had been of little value. As a woman, she felt that she would only fulfil her destiny if she produced a child, most especially a boy, and brought him up to continue her values and make her memories valuable. To her, childbearing was then the height of a woman's role. In a family like this, rural, pastoral, and wealthy, the routine work would have been done by paid servants or slaves. Therefore, as the eldest wife, her chief function would have been childbearing and child rearing. Further, in these communities, children were a sign of well-being, of wealth and prosperity, and they ensured the future. He was born because of agonizing prayer on the part of his childless mother, Hannah, who had been mocked by her husband Elkanah's other wife, Peninnah.

As he grew to manhood, it was clear that he was a man of God. Even as a child, God had spoken to him, and it was clear that he was being groomed to take over from the ailing and increasingly incompetent priest Eli, whose sons were so evil. Finally, as we shall see, it was after the Ark of the Covenant was captured and the old Eli died that Samuel took his place, and it was Samuel who would in turn appoint both Saul and David as kings, and while he lived the nation was relatively under the blessing of God.

Chapter 8
The Period of the Kings

After the nation of Israel had suffered so much from the surrounding nations, the situation was perilous. Failing, as they had, to destroy and eliminate the pagan tribes they were to replace, lacking any real substantial leadership for any consistent period, the nation was at the mercy of the resident tribes who saw them as invaders coming to seize their land and property. The most vigorous of their foes were the Philistines to the west, who themselves were trying to gain the fertile land formed by the wooded valleys whose streams fed the river Jordan. Whilst to the East they were challenged by the Midianites, who believed that by defeating the 'invading' Israelites would give them an opportunity to tackle the encroaching Philistines. Whilst the dominant need was to gain access to the fertile feeding grounds for their cattle and sheep.

What Israel believed it needed was a military leader, a king, who would unite the disparate tribes and lead them in battle to victory and re-establish the unity which had been lost when the country had been divided between the twelve tribes. Recognising Samuel as a 'man of God', one who could intercede with Him on their behalf, they approached Samuel with their request.

Samuel was bitterly disappointed by their request, seeing it as a challenge both to his position as a religious leader and as a personal rejection of his work and his life amongst them. To him it meant that they thought that he was a failure as a prophet and leader, and he complained bitterly to God about this. However, God's response was simply to tell him that it was not him, Samuel, that the people were rejecting, but Himself, their God. Not satisfied with the abstraction of a spiritual leader who made demands of holiness and respect but who could not be seen or, for that matter, understood. They wanted to be like the nations around them whose success lay in the hands of a strong military leader who led and controlled their lives.

Samuel was told to warn the nation of Israel that if they appointed a 'king', he would make demands on them. He would exercise the privilege of his position to demand military service from the men and domestic service from the women. He would take their money and their produce and demand payment to sustain a luxurious lifestyle. And that he would depend on them to do the manual work and for the men to be prepared to fight to the death if necessary. Most of all, unless the reigning king, their leader, was obedient to and responsive to God, they would lose the support of the one who by His power had so miraculously delivered them from 400 years of bondage, who had then supported them for 40 years in the desert, and whose promise to Abraham, their father, was the reason why they were there in the land and whose power, not their ability, had enabled them to achieve what they had.

Having warned the people, God allowed their request and chose for them a man whose appearance and background made him appear as a potential leader, and Samuel was told to anoint him with oil as a sign of God's blessing, and only then did he inform the man he had anointed with oil that he was God's choice to be the nation's king. The man was Saul, son of Kish.

Interestingly, God gave this chosen man a number of 'signs' that he had God's backing. Samuel told him that the donkeys he and his man were searching for had been found; he was told that he would meet a group of prophets and that he would join them in a holy dance.

But would the people accept this man? At first, they were dubious, but eventually, after witnessing Saul's military skill, the people did acclaim him as king. The story of how the prophet Samuel was used to appoint him as king and the consequences of his anointing are detailed in the chapters of the first book of Samuel.

Saul

Quite ironically, the increasing predatory incursions of Israel's long-term enemy, the Philistines, who occupied the coastal area of Canaan, was an important factor both in the appointment of a king and a major factor in uniting the nation behind him. Things came to a head when Israel went out to fight the Philistines, as described in Samuel chapter 4. In that battle the Ark of the Covenant, taken into battle to encourage the Israelite army, had been captured by the Philistines, and both of Eli's two sons were killed. Eli, their father, the priest, fell off his seat at the gate on hearing the news and died. The Philistines then took the Ark and put it in the temple of their god Dagon, and the ensuing detail is quite humorous. Their god fell over in front of the Ark, and when he was put back, he fell over again, and his head broke off. The Philistine nation moved to a different city, was smitten with disease, and their religious leaders blamed this on the presence of the Ark, and after a disastrous seven months, they sent it back to Israel. The full story is found in 1 Samuel chapter 5. However, when the Ark of the Covenant, Israel's Holy Place where God met with them, was returned, it was collected and taken to the house of Abinadab, where it stayed for twenty years until finally it was restored to its proper place, as we shall see later.

The Philistines, known as the Sea People because they occupied the coastal plain west of the Dead Sea, also known as the coastal trade route, the Way of the Sea, initially came from either Crete or Anatolia. They had previously been threatening the northern areas of Egypt in an endeavour to enlarge their territory until they were finally defeated under the reign of the Pharaoh Ramses III (1183–1152), as recorded on the walls of the temple at Medinat Habu. After which they appear to have turned to making incursions into Israeli territory, in the foothills of the mountains to the east of the coastal plain, and became a major problem to the Israelites for some 200 years, until they were defeated by the western thrusts of Assyria, a growing major force located east of the Euphrates which had, under their ruler Shalmaneser, occupied Syria and Damascus and would later become a major problem also for the nation of Israel.

Initially Saul was a good king, earning respect from his own people as well as an international reputation as a warrior. However, Israel at this time was facing their formidable opponent, the Philistines, who, at this time, occupied the crucial territory north of Egypt and along the coastal regions and, as we know, having been frustrated in their attempts to seize land from Egypt, were now attempting to extend their territory westwards into the land occupied by Israel.

The challenge the Philistines represented for Israel is nowhere more clearly seen than in the challenge of their heroic figure Goliath, who daily stood in front of their army and challenged the Israelites to single combat, the outcome to decide the fate of the losing nation. We must take account of the fact that, at this period, the Philistines had discovered the art of working with iron, a jealously guarded secret, whilst the Israelites were still in the 'bronze age'. It was at this point that a young shepherd boy distinguished himself. Sent by his father to check on his brothers who were soldiers in the Israelite army, he was appalled by the fact that a pagan champion should insult the God of Israel in such a manner, and he offered to face the Philistine alone and armed only with his shepherd's crook and his sling. That this young shepherd boy should be able to slay the giant soldier, with his iron plate armour and sword and spear, was startling evidence of how God's power was greater than the best of military might.

This story is so well known that I do not need to recount the details, which are recorded in 1 Samuel chapter 17. What is important is that following his remarkable success, Saul took the lad into his household, where he became a legend for his remarkable ability to fight so successfully. An ability which was obviously God-given. Typically, his valour and success were celebrated after every battle, to the extent that the young women sang, "Saul has slain his thousands, but David his tens of thousands." At this, Saul became increasingly jealous of the successes achieved by this lad, which included his ability to sing and play the harp, demonstrated later in his writing of the Psalms. All of which was compounded by his very close friendship with Saul's son Jonathan, who was Saul's presumptive heir, and later by his daughter Mical, who fell in love with David. The sad result of his jealousy was that he sought several times to kill David, until finally David was forced to flee and become a homeless outlaw, to be joined by a small but intensely loyal band of other men who were outcasts of society but who regarded David as a man of utter integrity and outstanding ability, and in turn they gave him their unswerving loyalty.

However, it was not simply this jealousy which brought about Saul's demise; he was also arrogant and infuriated his God when, for example, he flagrantly disobeyed a command from God related to him by the prophet Samuel. When Saul was sent to fight the Amalekites, he was told to utterly destroy them. But instead, he kept a large quantity of the spoil and did not kill Agag, their king. 1 Samuel 15. Now, with this flagrant example of disobeying God, his time was up. In His providence, for God is never taken unaware but knows what is in the future, the king in waiting was there, well trained militarily, totally responsive to God, not afraid to obey, whatever the cost. The ideal king.

Saul's final end, and that of his three sons, is described in 1 Samuel 31. They died as they and the Israeli army were defeated once again by the Philistines; David by this time was no longer in Saul's service, and Samuel the prophet had also died, much lamented, of old age, so that Israel was facing her enemies without God's help. The one I feel sorry for is Saul's eldest son and his heir,

Jonathan. For Jonathan loved David with a fierce loyalty, 'more than the love of a woman', and it was his intervention which enabled David to escape his father's wrath, even though in helping David, Jonathan knew that he was forfeiting his own claim to the throne. For David was God's choice. He died in battle with his father because, once again, despite his deep and close friendship with David, his place in extremity was beside his father. A man to be remembered for being true to himself and to God. The other person who loved him truly was Saul's daughter Michal, until she too became jealous of David's love for God. But after Saul's death, David insisted that she be restored to him, so no doubt David really loved her.

King David

When Samuel the prophet had been sent by God to the house of Jesse to anoint the new king, whom He had chosen to replace Saul, even he was surprised. The older brothers of the family were upstanding men who looked capable, but each one was rejected, and finally, when all seven had been rejected by God, the only one left was the youngest, who had been sent off to look after the family's sheep whilst his elders and betters met the prophet, the seer of such importance. However, God does not judge as others do, and He alone knew the future. But Samuel was told that this young lad was the one chosen by God, and he duly anointed him, and as he did so, the spirit of the Lord came upon David and departed from Saul. 1 Samuel 16:13–14. Samuel himself was in a dilemma, because if the news got out, his own life as well as that of God's chosen replacement would be in danger. And David was at this time just a lad, but a very talented one.

However, things were about to change for King Saul, and the change came in the form of an evil spirit which came upon him. Once again, we can see evidence of the negative, evil force which is always present whenever people fail God. In this case it was Saul's disobedience to God's command which was the root cause. For his servants the solution to the problem was music, and that meant young David, who was described by Saul's servants as "a mighty valiant man, cunning in playing music, a man of war, and good-looking."

However, now the saga really began, for not only was David a calming influence on Saul, but his remarkable talents, exercised under the direction and power of God following his anointing by Samuel, singled him out above all other men around Saul. Just as had happened with Joseph, hated and sold by his brothers when he had been imprisoned. And as had happened to many other people who had been chosen by God for a specific purpose. But, as David's charisma increased, Saul, originally himself an outstanding man, diminished. God's favour had departed. First it was David's unbelievable success against the giant Goliath, whose challenge had defied both God and the Israelite army. Then it was David's success as a military leader and the public acclaim he won, which rankled and bitterly increased Saul's jealousy but which inspired Jonathan's love, and now his ability as a musician.

Once again, we have a clear picture of the manner in which God's blessing upon a simple human can raise him to eminence and power, whilst the loss of that power would diminish and reduce a man who had begun so valiantly and with great success. No wonder Paul would later add, "We have this treasure in earthen vessels, that the excellence of the power might be of God and not of man." 2 Corinthians 4:7. It was the same with men like Gideon, raised from humble status to heroic heights by the power of God. One can name so many in scripture: Abraham, Samuel, Elijah, and through to the saints and heroes of the New Testament, of whom Paul is possibly one of the finest examples. And it can happen today, because the 'evidence' of God is seen so often when ordinary people perform heroic tasks.

The tragedy for Saul was that his jealousy led him to persecute and seek to kill David, whilst for David, his exploits in exile would endear him to the men who were with him and pave the way for him to become their favourite king of all time. So much so that Jesus Himself would later be described as "great David's great son." When, finally, after Saul's tragic death with his sons, the men of his own tribe, Judah, accepted him as their king, he would rule in the South over the tribes of Benjamin and Judah for some three and a half years before finally the Northern kingdom tribes would approach him and accept his role as their king. And so, for his final thirty-three years, he was king over the whole nation of Israel. And what a king he became. Victorious militarily and loved even by other nations whom he had defeated in battle, as well as by his own people, he united the nation and made it a nation which was respected by all the surrounding nations. To such an extent that, when he died, his son Solomon would reap the reward and make the Israelite nation one of the most wealthy and respected in the whole of that region, ensuring peace.

However, David was not without faults; no one is. His main faults were in two areas. First, his love for Bathsheba, the wife of Uriah the Hittite, which led him to commit adultery and, when she became pregnant, to commit murder by sentencing her husband, Uriah, to be sacrificed in war. Yet God was merciful, and ultimately it was her second child, Solomon, the first child, the one born of adultery, having died, who was to become king after David.

However, even more alarming was the fact that one of his sons, Absalom, rebelled against him. Absalom would not only proclaim himself king and force his father to flee the city, but also he would bring civil war between his supporters and those loyal to the king. Then, when Absalom was killed in battle, David's grief at his death nearly lost him the kingdom altogether. 2 Samuel 18:33. Then too, there were issues over David's successor. His son Adonijah, the eldest, proclaimed himself king, and it was only the presence of mind of Zadoc the priest and Nathan the prophet, who alerted Bathsheba, who reminded the king of his promise that Solomon, her son, should be king, which saved the day. The other fault was David's action in numbering the people, which led to God's punishment. Gad the prophet gave David the choice of three things. 2 Samuel 24:12–15. Seven years of famine, three months of defeat at the hand of his enemies, or three days of pestilence in the land. David chose to fall into the hands of God, the third option, and the nation was finally spared when David admitted his sin and offered a sacrifice at the threshing floor of Araunah, who offered him the land free of charge, but David's famous words, "Why should I offer the Lord that which hath cost me naught led to his paying Araunah either 50 shekels of silver, as in verse 24, or the much larger sum of 600 gold coins, as told in 1 Chronicles 21:24."

So what was it that led to David being described as 'a man after God's own heart'? Was it his ability as a soldier, his loving nature as revealed in his affection for Jonathan, or his ability to unite those twelve very different tribes? None of these; it was the fact that, in spite of his human failings, he loved God with all his heart and was not ashamed to show it. As is so poignantly revealed in the remarkably expressive psalms in the Bible, of which he is believed to have written half. It is these writings which most clearly reveal his inner feelings, his love for and trust in God. They were composed during the time of some of his most tempestuous moments, and they demonstrate both his ability to express his gratitude to God and his ability to describe for us his relationship with Him. These are very human emotive factors which we, today, find so demonstrative of his love for God and, in return, the comfort and blessing he received from Him. And revealing his desire for God's guidance at every step of the journey.

Today we find them so very relevant to our situation; they are so up-to-date. Because he expresses the same emotions which fill our lives today. Words such as "The Lord is my shepherd; I shall not want" show a man who loved God with all his heart and who is experiencing a deep and close relationship with his God. Even in the middle of his exile and later during his battles with his enemies and the betrayal of his closest friends and his own family, they reveal his own deepest thoughts. These are David's prayers, in which he expresses his love for God and his worship. They are honest expressions of his inner emotions, as he challenges God and questions what is happening to him and why. Overall they are a record of David's deep love for God and his confidence in God's justice, whatever happens.

Written, as these songs and poems were, some nine hundred years before the time of Christ, I cannot think of any writer of the period or for many centuries later who has been able to express so clearly his own personal feelings. Here we have first-hand expressions of deeply personal feelings, written whilst the feelings were still raw, still vivid in the mind of the writer, and therefore extremely powerful and immediate. They are the work of a man inspired.

This is true of many of the other so-called 'poetic works'. The book of Job, for example, may be seen as attempting to find the same answers as the Greek poets and philosophers of that period. Basically, described in the opening two chapters as a dispute between God and Satan over the underlying reason for Job's devout worship, it then completely changes direction and becomes a debate between Job and his three friends. They claim that his misfortunes are the result of a sinful life and therefore are justly the punishment of God. They warn him that the only solution to his miserable condition is not to end it all but to repent, because God is a God of Justice and may well forgive him. However, Job maintains his innocence, as is explicit in the opening chapter. It ends with Job being challenged to understand how infinite God's knowledge and power are as the great creator, and he is told to forgive and pray for his friends, and when he does that, his fortunes are reversed, and he spends his last 140 years as a prosperous family man again. The work entitled 'The Song of Solomon' is another of these remarkably insightful poems, which explores so delicately the emotions of two people who are deeply in love. It is included here because the compilers of the original scriptures saw it as a symbolic parable, defining the love between mankind and God. And therefore, of value to readers.

King Solomon

After his father's death, his son Solomon was anointed as king. This was both David's own wish and the fulfilment of a promise to his mother, Bathsheba. But it was not without some controversy, because Adonijah, the eldest son, had already had himself crowned, but supported only by Joab, one of the leading men of the army. However, David himself intervened, and Solomon was formally anointed as successor, and this appointment was supported by all the leading men and by Zadoc the priest and Nathan the prophet. 1 Kings chapters 1 and 2. The choice was without doubt the right one because under Solomon the kingdom prospered, and David's wish to build a temple worthy of the worship of the creator God was fulfilled.

At the start of his reign, Solomon was greatly blessed by God. He received the gift of great wisdom, which was outstanding for his time, and this made him a man of international fame (1 Kings 4:29–34). An example of his wisdom is given to us in the decision to the 2 prostitutes. 1 Kings 3:16–28. Through his leadership, the kingdom prospered and became extremely wealthy and secure. However, he would fall from grace because in later life he turned from wholehearted loyalty to God through his multiple marriages to foreign wives, beginning with his marriage to the daughter of the king of Egypt, 1 Kings 3:1. These women brought with them the customs and false worship of their native lands, and we find Solomon allowing them to pursue the worship of their ancestors, even to allowing them to place idols to false gods in the Temple. Which resulted in utter chaos in the country on his death. Evidence that the prosperity and wealth were conditional upon his total commitment to the way of God, 1 Kings 2:3–4.

The life of Solomon, his building of the magnificent Temple, and his success in leading the nation were seen to be examples of God's blessing, which remained with Solomon, despite his failings in later years, because of God's promise to David that his heirs would inherit the kingdom. The ultimate heir being Jesus, 'great David's greater son'. The sheer stupidity of Solomon's son Rehoboam in alienating the ten Northern tribes is described in 1 Kings 12. In disgust they chose instead a vagabond named Jeroboam (1 Kings 12:16–20 and never again would the kingdom be fully united, because within a few years, to avoid the people going to the Temple in Jerusalem to worship, other places of worship, and with them other gods, were set up in the Northern cities.

What a disaster for the once very powerful nation. Everything about this nation was a totally conditional one. It depended on the total commitment of the people and their full obedience to the laws of God. And this was amply demonstrated by the history of that nation. Its message to individuals and the nations of the world is that 'With God all things are possible', but, without God, man left to his own resources will fail. Simply because human nature is basically self-centred and self-serving, seeking power over itself and others, which makes the laws of God unacceptable. Remember the adage, 'All power corrupts, absolute power corrupts absolutely'.

So, the nation is divided into two. The larger, Northern kingdom, first under the leadership of Jeroboam, son of Nebat, becomes corrupt. The worship of God was discarded in favour of the gods of the surrounding nations whom they had been told to drive out. Some of their kings did pay attention to the law of God, but most of them, like the notorious Ahab and his wife Jezebel, were extreme in their opposition both to God and to the prophets and priests whom He sent. The most remarkable of these prophets was Elijah, who challenged and defeated the prophets of Baal, as we shall see later, but any triumph was short-lived until, weakened by successive wars and unable to win their many battles, as a nation they were finally overrun and conquered by the dominant Assyrians in 722 BC (2 Kings 17:22–26). Of the kings succeeding Jeroboam, the worst was probably Ahab, who was driven by his wife, Jezebel, to outlaw true religious values and follow the worship of Baal. Of the kings succeeding Jeroboam, only Jehu could be classed as good; apart from him, they all continued the worship of other gods, which led finally to the downfall of the nation.

This account of the Northern tribes is not about individuals; it is the account of the decline of a nation which deliberately ignored the basic rules set out by God for the benefit of the whole community. Individuals there were who stood out against the evils of their day, most notable the prophets like Samuel, Elijah, and his successor Elisha, but their influence was short-lived, overwhelmed by corrupt leadership. The fate of this once proud nation, whose achievements under God had been enormous, is indicative of society today, where every advancement of science becomes an opportunity for vice and immorality. Social media sites, which are exploited by criminals and which are used to corrupt young minds. Society needs strong leadership, yes, but if that society and its leaders ignore the basic rules as outlined for the Israelite nation, those nations will decline morally and socially as personal gain overtakes communal standards.

The Southern kingdom of Judah, which also included the tribe of Benjamin, whose territory was to the south of Judah, was always more loyal to their ancestor David. Remember that after Saul's death they were the first to acknowledge David as their king, and it was a further seven years before the Northern tribes recognized him and valued what he stood for. Those values were discarded by Solomon's son Rehoboam, and it was the total rejection of these values by Rehoboam which resulted in the Northern tribes breaking away from Judah and, with it, their distancing from the Temple, which stood in Jerusalem as the focal point of their community life. In the same way today, it is the increasing decline of church attendance, or more pointedly, the decline in the influence of the church in our modern society, which reflects the ascendency of the other values. Those of self-esteem, self-indulgence, and self-gratification. A moral decline which, fundamentally, is to some extent the result of the decline in spirituality of the churches. In the case of the ten Northern tribes after the southern two tribes were able to hold on to their values for another one hundred years, until 586/7, largely the result of the reforms carried out by some of their kings. Most notably Joash and Hezekiah and, to a lesser extent, Amaziah and Uzziah, but finally as a nation, they too succumbed to the Babylonians, under Nebuchadnezzar, who were replacing the Assyrians as the dominant force in West Euphrates.

The demise of these two kingdoms was not a sudden affair; it was the result of a series of battles and resulting loss of territory as the two nations declined in power spiritually and consequently militarily and socially, leaving us with a permanent record of the way in which a nation's relationship with God lies at the heart of its success or lack of it. For a much more detailed account of this period, complete with details of the major battles and the location of the attacking forces, see "The Readers Digest Maps of the Holy Land," which goes into great detail. This was not a time of individual failure so much as a disastrous period of leadership. However, from the time of the Judges, God had kept His witness. The prophet Samuel it was who had anointed both Saul and David, under the guidance of God. After his death, David was guided by prophets like Nathan and Gad, but over the years, two men stand out: Elijah and his successor, Elisha.

Chapter 9
The Prophets

Elijah and Elisha

Elijah and Elisha were very different characters. Elijah, a solitary man, dressed rather as John the Baptist would later dress. In fact, at one time during his ministry, it was thought that John the Baptist was a reincarnation of Elijah, whose main encounter was with the King Ahab and his notorious wife Jezebel. It was not enough that Jezebel worshipped both Baal and Ashtoreth, but she had appointed four hundred and fifty and four hundred prophets in number to conduct and promote their worship. God sent Elijah to challenge Ahab by sending a three-year drought on the land (1 Kings 18).

What is so remarkable about Elijah is his absolute faith in God and his willingness to put his life on the line to demonstrate God's power over nature as well as over humanity. At his word, God withholds rain for three years, reducing the whole nation to desperation. At that very moment, when the whole country is looking for a solution, even the king is out looking for water to feed their animals; they are given two alternatives. Jezebel's 450 prophets of Baal and her 400 prophets of the female goddess Ashtaroth or the single figure of a man of God. The challenge was to get their respective gods or God to react, to answer. The challenge was to build an altar and then ask their god to set fire to it.

The prophets of Baal have the first go, but whilst Elijah laughs at them and mocks them, perhaps your god is away or even relieving himself. Then at the appointed time for the Israelite God's worship, Elijah's simple prayer causes fire to come from heaven and burn up the water thrown on the wood, the offering, and the stones from which the altar was built. In the excitement and wonder at this stupendous miracle, Elijah orders the death of all the false prophets, but he then has to pray for the real answer to the problem afflicting the nation, rain. And in answer to his prayer, God does send rain, with a cloud on the horizon the 'size of a man's hand'. At this simple sign, in faith he tells the king Ahab to hurry home, or he will get very wet. James, in Chapter 5 of his letter, says simply that "Elijah was a man of like passions as we are, yet he prayed earnestly that it might not rain, and there was a drought for three years." In other words, he experienced all the emotions that we experience. After his great victory at Mt. Carmel, he suffered greatly from anxiety and fear at Jezebel's threats. He also thought that he was alone, the only person left to challenge the evils of his society, and had to be reminded that God had reserved seven thousand men who had not bowed the knee to Baal when finally he met with God on Mt. Sinai, 1 Kings 19:10–18.

It was his absolute faith which meant that Elijah joins Moses as they speak with Jesus at His transfiguration. His absolute faith marks him out as a unique character but also as a man whose faith in God was to influence the lives of a nation and bring about the fall of a king, Ahab, and his even more evil queen, Jezebel. He was a giant of faith who challenged the evils of the society of his day, but he was also a humble and deeply emotional person and suffered accordingly. Yet his reward was God's approval. There are few examples of miracles which he performed, but his successor, Elisha, recognized his great influence when he asked, as Elijah was about to be taken up to heaven, for a share of the power which he and others recognized in him, and he calls him, "Mighty defender of Israel."

By contrast, Elisha performs more recorded miracles, most notably his healing of the Syrian army chief, Naaman, from his leprosy (2 Kings 5) and his gift of a son to the childless rich woman at Shunem who has built him a place to stay on the roof of her house, and then when that child died, he raised him to life again. 2 Kings 4:12. From our point of view, these were two major figures challenging the morally sick nation of Israel, the Northern kingdom, larger than the Southern part with its ten tribes and fundamentally stronger and more wealthy that their Southern neighbours, but also the first to be destroyed as God called them to account.

These two men, Elijah and Elisha, were typical of ordinary men who became the 'sons of God'. Ordinary men who became filled with the spirit and power of the living God, men who by their outstanding lives not only set an example of godly living but were also able to communicate with God, and through them God was able to reveal Himself to humanity. As the two nations, Judah, from which the modern name, Jews, is derived, and Israel, the larger ten tribes of the North, became forgetful of their history, the account of their ancestry and the way in which God had formed them into the most powerful nation in that area remains as a vital record. God sent these men, and many like them, to reprove, rebuke, and foretell the future. The kings who listened, as David did to Samuel and then to Nathan and Gad, prospered. Whilst those who refused to listen saw their nations decline in importance until, finally, they were overthrown. Israel by the Assyrians and Judah by the Babylonians. Finally, as we shall see, Judah was allowed to return under the Persians, who had replaced the Assyrians as the dominant power in the area, but not the ten tribes which formed the nation of Northern Israel.

However, the reign of the kings of both nations after David's son Solomon, whom God supported despite his declining faithfulness to God's covenant because of His promise to David that his descendants should occupy the throne, was a sorry story of unbelief, idolatry, and disobedience. Until, finally, God had had enough and once again allowed their enemies to overrun them. Which meant 70 years in exile, followed by some 400 years of relative independence under successive rulers, such as the Maccabee family, until the Romans stepped in and reoccupied their land to quell the series of rebellious actions. And that was the situation when Jesus was born. He lived in an occupied country. The overlords being the Romans, who allowed a degree of autonomy to the religious leaders.

It was Roman policy to allow their various conquered nations to be responsible for local affairs and used some of them to collect the local taxes, of whom Matthew the disciple was one, but this nation had a reputation for rebellious behaviour. Which was why the occupying Romans had built a fort inside the city and installed a local governor, Pontius Pilate, under whose authority the Jews were allowed to crucify Jesus. As we know from history, this rebellious situation continued for a further thirty-odd years after Jesus' death until the situation became so bad that the Roman Emperor, Vespasian, ordered his son Titus to besiege the city and destroy it.

After a three-year siege, which reduced the inhabitants to utter despair, the city finally fell in AD 70, and Titus then destroyed everything, including the Temple built by Herod, and exiled all of its citizens, again, leaving the city desolate and mostly under the control of the Turks for 2,000 years, until May 8th, 1948, when the modern state of Israel was established under the reorganization of Europe after the Second World War.

Sadly, the Western world has followed a similar pattern. Following the success of the Apostles after the time of Christ, the message of the Gospel spread throughout the Roman Empire, only to suffer badly as the years passed and other religions like Islam took their place. And then the so-called 'age of reason', when science began to explore and explain a different view of the universe, one which posited the idea that over vast eons of time the universe and human life had evolved without any supernatural force, as men like Charles Darwin in the 19th century produced their theories. It was then, with the decline of Christian ideals, that came the decline in moral standards and the overthrow of belief in things like a time of future Judgement. Wealth, luxury, and licentiousness became the goals for the wealthy, whilst with the coming of the industrial revolution the role of the ordinary people became less important, as machinery replaced the cottage industry of manual labour, whilst on the farms increasing mechanization would replace much of the manual labour. The result was poverty, hunger, and despair, as women and children were employed in the cotton and woollen factories and even in the mines to work long hours for a mere pittance of pay until Christian men like Lord Shaftesbury would introduce the factory acts, forbidding children under the age of six or seven from being employed. But, until men like Robert Raikes began to introduce free schooling, the gap between those who were wealthy and could afford an education and the rest widened to a great gulf.

It was into this scenario that the great Christian leaders were born. Men like William Booth, who revolutionised work amongst the poor and utterly destitute millions whose depravity was a scar on the face of Victorian England, as a century earlier the brothers John and Charles Wesley had not only reinvigorated a moribund Church but, potentially, by their work, forestalled in England the social revolution which would ravage France and destroy its monarchy at the end of the 18th century. Now, after so much revival of the Christian religion in the 18th and 19th centuries, in this country we appear once again to be living in a period of unrestricted, unchallenged licentiousness, against which the Church of today seems to be powerless, as a new scientific electronic age permits the pursuit of the black forces which are destroying our society and our children.

People call themselves Christian simply because they endeavour to follow the practices of religious worship, in which their religious belief is reduced to a formal recognition of the age-old principles without recognizing the Almighty and supernatural power of the living God. As Paul will deride them as "having a form of godliness but denying the power thereof." 2 Timothy 3:5.av. What we need today is a renewal of faith, conviction of sin under the power of the Holy Spirit, and a return to the fundamental truths of Holy Scripture, the Word of God.

Revival, in other words, and for that we need committed, dedicated, and faithful men and women of God. The alternative is an increasing decline to a day when God has to intervene with a day of Judgement. Jesus did warn that before He returns there will be a "falling away" from the truth and power of what He taught. Are we now in the middle of what Revelation calls the time of Tribulation, which immediately precedes our Lord's return?

Isaiah and Jeremiah

It is at this point that we can see that in the Old Testament the nation of Israel had departed so far from their covenant with God that he became sickened even by the insincerity of their worship, as depicted in Isaiah 29:11–14. What happened for Israel was that God sent a series of prophets to warn the nations by calling them to repent, to return to their true worship, to get rid of all idolatry, and to worship in sincerity. As Jesus said to the woman at the well of Sychar, "The time is come, and now is when they who worship God must worship Him in sincerity and truth, for the father seeketh such to worship Him." John 4:23 A.v.

The two prophets, Isaiah and Jeremiah, were the two leading prophets who were chosen by God to warn the nations of their impending doom. Isaiah was a simple man but one who was specifically chosen by God for the purpose, and he is shown to have been a quite remarkable person. Not just in the scope of his prophetic utterances, the breadth of his vision, and the extent of the period he covered. He was also a prolific writer whose language and powers of expression are legendary. However, his role in the history of Israel is quite unique because he foretold of a future glory for the nation, and it is this hope which still inspires the nation and is one reason for their continued existence.

Look at these words, written when the nation was in deep distress: "The Lord is bringing on you, on your people, and on the whole royal family, days of trouble worse than any that have come." Isaiah 7:17. But also, "Must you wear out the patience of people – must you wear out God's patience too? Well then, The Lord Himself will give you a sign: a young woman who is pregnant will have a son and will name him 'Immanuel'." God is with us. Isaiah 7:14. "But the future will bring honour to this region, from the Mediterranean Eastwards to the land on the other side of Jordan and even to Galilee itself." Isaiah 9:1. "A child is born to us! A son is given to us! And He will be our ruler. He will be called 'Wonderful', Counsellor, Mighty God, Eternal Father, and Prince of Peace'. His royal power will continue to grow; His kingdom will always be at peace. He will rule as King David's successor…from now until the end of time." And this is exactly what the Israelites were looking for and, to this day, continue to expect.

The problems underlying their failure to recognize Jesus of Nazareth lay first in that, according to Micah 3:2, the Messiah was to be born in Bethlehem, and the people thought that Jesus was born in Nazareth, but equally they could not come to terms with the concept of the suffering servant of Isaiah 52 and 53. This was not compatible with their understanding of Great David's Son, coming to deliver their nation from the oppressor. In this case, the authority of Rome.

True religious Jews are still to this day waiting for the return of their Messiah, having so dramatically rejected Him when he first came. A mistake which to us seems almost unbelievable. But the great interest for us who are 'Gentiles' by birth is that the New Testament believers were also promised that He would return, and it is this expectation which has fired the Church through the centuries and inspires both hope and belief, as we shall see later.

The prophet Jeremiah is notable really for two things. First, that his message was chiefly to the kings and the people in the years leading up to and including the destruction of Jerusalem and the exile into Babylonia. Warning them of the perils of their situation and living to see his predictions fulfilled. He used a lot of very plain language, warning of the grave errors of idolatry (3:19ff) and calling the people to repent before it was too late. But he was also remarkable because of his own personal involvement. He suffered with the people during the invasions and battles, weeping and sick at heart (8:18ff) and enacting some dramatic scenes of distress, such as his visit to the Potter's house (Ch. 18). And the basket of figs, 24. And he symbolically wears an ox yoke, 27:1. But he was also heavily criticised for being too pessimistic in his warnings, whereas actually he was being totally realistic, as events proved. But his warnings resulted in his being imprisoned, put in a dry well, and nearly died. However, like Isaiah, he did foretell a more hopeful future, Ch. 23, with the news that God would establish the rule of a righteous descendant of David, 23:5, who would be called "The Lord our Salvation." 23:6, but his account does not have the detail provided by Isaiah. He also told that Israel would return home (Ch. 31), and he warned many other nations of God's coming judgement on them. Ironically, he was released from prison by the Babylonian Nebuchnezzar and allowed to rejoin his own people, who were still left in Judah.

Ezekiel and Daniel

Of the other prophets, the two most important were first Ezekiel, who lived in exile in Babylonia both before the captivity and during it. Like Isaiah and Jeremiah before him, Ezekiel had been specifically called by God to warn Israel of their impending punishment. 2:1. And it ends with the vision of a New Jerusalem and a new Temple.

The main burden of the prophet Daniel was a series of visions and miraculous encounters during the exile under Babylon and Persia. The miraculous encounters involve Daniel and his three colleagues, Shadrach, Meshach, and Abednego, who were amongst the leading citizens taken by the Babylonians to train as leaders of their own people. However, they maintained their loyalty to their Jewish sacred customs, which involved their insisting on avoiding the rich food of their Babylonian counterparts, living a 'separate' life, and refusing to worship the Emperor's golden image. The three were thrown into a 'burning fiery furnace' and emerged unscathed, having said that their God could deliver them, but even if He didn't they still would not worship the image. And Daniel himself was thrown into a den of lions because, contrary to the king's decree, he prayed daily to his God. He then emerged, totally unharmed, to the amazement of the authorities. The visions which Daniel was able to interpret told of the end of Belshazzar's life, and then he described in detail the symbolic relevance of the destruction of Nebuchadnezzar's great image, through which God foretold the end of all those empires which were oppressing the Israelites. Media, Persia, Greece, and Rome.

These four prophets were each chosen specifically by God for a major purpose. Isaiah and Jeremiah to warn the two kingdoms of their coming exile, under Syria and Babylon respectively, because of their disobedience and idolatry and their continued refusal to change, to repent, and to reform. But both of these prophets also spoke of a time of great restoration, and this is where the symbolism is so vital, because it told of the coming of Jesus, the Son of the most high God. But it also told of His suffering and death at the hands of His own people, which would result in 2,000 years of tragedy for Israel. And this is what the Jews of His day could not understand. Neither could they anticipate the reality. No longer just the 430 years of slavery in Egypt and forty years adrift in the wilderness, nor the 70 years of exile in Babylonia, but a prolonged period of some 2,000 years of exile from their promised land. Something which we have seen fulfilled historically. And it is here, in the Bible, that we can see the future of a universal kingdom and a future ahead for the whole world. The whole of this vast universe will come under the sovereignty and rule of the King of Kings. Which was the original plan of God and the reason why God has created our world. But the rest of the answer can only be seen in Part 2.

The Children of God Part 2
The New Testament

Introduction

There are some four hundred and fifty years between the last book of the Old Testament, Malachi, and the beginning of the New Testament, during which time there had been several major political developments over the whole of that area known as West Euphrates. Not least was the fact that Rome had now replaced the Persians as the major power in that area, and they had also defeated the old, long-established Egyptian regime, which had, from time to time, been a refuge for persecuted Israelis. However, to understand the internal political situation in Israel at the time of the New Testament, we need to understand what had happened in those very turbulent years between the end of Persian dominance of the area, which had led to the return of the Jews and the rebuilding of their Temple, up to the situation under Roman occupation. This will help us to understand the situation in Israel at the time of our Lord's birth. Because these factors, which will set the scene, socially and politically, of the world into which Jesus came, will have a very strong influence on forthcoming events.

The Israeli nation had had a long history of rebellious behaviour, made evident first in their attitude towards their God. Right from the time of their release from Egypt, they were forever complaining about their food, about a lack of water, and even against the leadership of Moses and Aaron. As for example, in Exodus chapters 17 and 32 and Numbers 14, to the extent that twice God had threatened to destroy them and begin again with Moses. In later years, the same rebelliousness was there, both internally under their own leaders, the Maccabees, and later under the domination of occupying forces. It was this factor which influenced the local King, Herod, to build a fort within the city walls and maintain a garrison there, and it was the nation's past turbulent history which would make the Romans fear further insurrection. This is why Jesus was seen by them as yet another potential troublemaker, as later the Apostle Paul would face the same accusation in Jerusalem, Acts 21:38.

The Old Testament ends with the very slow progress being made by the returning Jews under the orders of the Persian emperors, Cyrus and Darius. During the Persian period, the returning Jews had been led by men like Ezra and Nehemiah. Ezra was a Hebrew scholar well briefed in the Law who had been one of the exiles, and Nehemiah had been an official working in Persia under Darius, and he was now in Jerusalem, acting under his authority.

However, during this interim period, vast political changes took place in the area known as West Euphrates. The dominant Persians, who had replaced both the Assyrians and the Babylonians, had in turn been routed by the Macedonians under their leader, Alexander the Great, in 333 BC, who, after his father's death in 335 BC, would then succeed his father as head of state. Alexander's illustrious career had led him to achieve conquest over an empire which stretched from India to Egypt. He had freely travelled via the Way of the Sea, which was the main coastal road through what we know as Palestine, but he did not attack the Israeli city of Jerusalem. The Israeli state, part of what was called Canaan, was at that time ruled by a local Hebrew tribe, the Maccabees, and because the Israelis were not impeding his progress, he left them in peace.

After Alexander's death, at age 33, the area had been fought over again. This time by Greek forces, under men like Ptolemy and Antigonus, who were also contending with the vast Egyptian state, which, as we well know, had been so powerful for some 3,000 years. Israel again suffered less from this conflict, even though its territory lay on the direct route along the coastal highway, which gave access to Egypt, which nation was now a declining force. In fact, under Ptolemaic rule, Israel was relatively peaceful. In 198 BC, Antiochus III had in fact assisted in the reconstruction of the Temple in Jerusalem, most probably to encourage loyalty from the ruling but very troublesome Maccabees.

Sadly, as time passed, the land of Israel would become a battleground between the armies of the declining Greeks and the forces of the new power, which was becoming dominant in the area, Rome. A conflict which would end the years of Egyptian greatness. One of the Roman generals, Anthony, in his pursuit of power in Rome, allied himself with the last Egyptian ruler, Cleopatra, but they lost out, being defeated at the naval battle of Actium, and Egypt's power was then finished with Cleopatra's death. Subsequently, Jerusalem itself came under attack and fell to Roman troops under Herod around 38 BC. However, Herod had followed the Roman custom of encouraging local loyalty in conquered areas by rebuilding the Jewish Temple in Jerusalem. This had been reconstructed during the struggling formative years of the Jewish return and rebirth under Persian rule. But it had never achieved the majesty of the original, which had been planned by King David and built at the height of Israel's power by David's son, Solomon. Now, the Temple, rebuilt by Herod, was once again an object of admiration, which caught the attention of Jesus' disciples when they pointed it out to Him from the Mount of Olives. Although Jesus knew more about it than they ever did, having spent time there during His childhood.

One other thing we must recognize, in order to understand the background to the period of our Lord's life, is that the years under the Maccabees had been a very turbulent period. They were nationalistic, yes, but they were trying to replace the worship of Israel's God Jehovah with the worship of the pagan god Zeus, which was bitterly opposed by the priesthood. And, as nationalists, they were always troublesome to any occupying force. For this reason, the Romans, when they occupied the land, had built a fortress within the walls of the city, and one can see the political force of Caiaphas' statement as he proposed the death of Jesus, "Better that one man die than the whole nation suffer." And to the Roman soldiers, Jesus was yet another revolutionary. This also accounts for the fact that some thirty years later, in AD 70, the Romans, finally tired of its rebellion, besieged the city, which had defied them, captured and occupied it, and exiled all its original inhabitants. They had finally had enough. What happened to the nation of Israel after this is common history, which we shall examine later.

It is important for us to understand what had happened to the nation of Israel between the promise which God gave to Abraham that He would give his, Abraham's, descendants possession of their own country and that He would drive out their enemies and sustain them and the birth of Jesus. Because Jesus was there, although not recognized as such, to become the fulfilment of so many prophetic forecasts made in their historical records. This Promise had been originally made to Abraham, then called Abram, some 2,000 years before the time of Christ, as recorded in Genesis 11:31. Where we are told that Terah, his father, had taken Abram, his son, and his grandson Lot, his brother Haran's son, and, together with all their possessions, they went from Ur, the Chaldean city in Babylonia, where they had been living, to settle far to the West in a hilly but fertile area known as Canaan, where the father, Terah, died. God had already spoken to Abram, telling him to leave his father and kindred to live in a land which He, God, would show him, Genesis 12:1, promising that He would make of Abram a great nation and mightily bless him and his descendants. So off went Abram, now 75 years of age, taking his nephew Lot with him. But both men were wealthy, with flocks and herds, and their herdsmen quarrelled over their respective rights to pasture and water. So, they decided to separate the families. Lot chose to go down into the very fertile Jordan valley, whilst Abram stayed in the hill country.

After some ten years the Lord appeared again to Abram and renewed His promise to make him the head of a great family. Abram's response was that he was childless, and his property would therefore go to his chief Steward. In a great vision, the Lord promised Abram that his own child would be the one to inherit. To resolve this problem, during the intervening years, Sarai had given her maid, Hagar, to Abram, and she bore him a child, whom she named Ishmael. But that was a human action and was not the answer, which would be a Divine miracle. Then, as Genesis 17 explains, when Abram was 99 years of age, the Lord appeared to him again to tell him that Sarai, his wife, would bear a child, even though she was about 80 years of age. To confirm the Covenant with Abram, God insisted that every male child born to the family should be circumcised at eight days, and He renamed Abram, Abraham, and Sarai, Sarah. The child, born in due course, was named Isaac, who, in turn, was the father of Jacob.

Jacob then, having been told in a vision to return to the old family home in Mesopotamia, where he married the two daughters of his uncle Laban and became the father of 12 sons, who would become the heads of twelve tribal clans. Then a most severe famine struck the whole region, one which would last for seven years. But, in God's miraculous provision, one of Jacob's sons, Joseph, had been sold as a slave into Egypt, where, under God's mercy and guidance, he became a great leader, second only to the Pharaoh in authority. But this was most fortuitous, because, having such authority, he was able to save his own family from the prolonged famine, which afflicted Canaan as well as Egypt, and enabled that family, initially of just 70 persons, to live and work in Goshen in the Nile Delta, where they would prosper and develop numerically into a nation of some two million people over the next 430 years, as we have seen in Exodus 12: 37–40. But, over the years, they became seen as a potential threat to Egypt's security and were reduced to the status as slaves to keep them under control. But, despite God's help, the nation continually failed to live up to God's required standard of obedience and worship as required by the terms of the Covenant God had made with Abraham. Consequently, despite some remarkable moments of supernatural success, including their miraculous escape from Egypt and the destruction of the pursuing Egyptian army at the Red Sea, they never achieved the original goal which God had set them. After suffering forty years wandering in the desert and having been miraculously supplied by God, when they finally entered the land under the leadership of Joshua, they never became a truly God-fearing nation. They worshipped other gods and intermarried with the native people they were told to drive out. God's plan for them had always been that in the future, they would become an everlasting kingdom, obedient to the laws of God, ruled by a descendant of their great King David, and being an example of God's love and goodness to the rest of the world. Hence their troubled situation when Jesus was born. A nation of great potential which had failed because of disobedience. However, as we know, Jesus, who was the Son of God, became for a while the Son of Man, born of Mary, so that He might become God's answer to human failure through His infinite mercy and love and His redeeming, atoning death on the Cross. But that never happened, because they failed to recognize who He was, and, in ignorance, they killed the one who would have delivered them.

Chapter 1
The Beginning Of the Drama

John The Baptist

The first indication that things were about to change came when a fiery preacher began a crusade in and around the capital, Jerusalem, speaking mostly in the desert areas and on the banks of the river Jordan. His message was simply, "Turn away from your sins because the Kingdom of heaven is near." The interesting thing is that quite a number of people did believe him and were baptized by him in the river Jordan as a sign of their repentance. But John insisted that he was not the expected Messiah of prophetic vision. He said that "The man who will come after me is much greater than I am. I baptize you with water, but He will baptize you with the Holy Spirit." It is Luke in his gospel who tells us most about John the Baptist and his preaching and the fact that he angered Herod the governor because John had rebuked him over the fact that he had married Herodias, his brother's wife, and done many evil things. Which is why later we find that Herod had him put in prison and will later behead him at the whim of his daughter Salome, acting on behalf of her mother, Herodias.

We know little of the early years of this man, who was in fact related to Jesus through their mothers. Luke, in his Gospel, goes into detail to tell us how John was born, miraculously, to aged priestly parents, Zechariah and his wife Elizabeth, in a manner rather like the birth of Isaac to Abraham and Sarah all those years earlier. The same messenger from God, Gabriel, was sent six months later to tell a young girl, Mary, that she was to become the mother of the Messiah, who was to be named Jesus. What we do know is that John's parents were very elderly when he was born, so that at the time he began his ministry he would have been roughly the same age as Jesus, who had been born six months later, thirty years. It is likely that his parents had died soon after his birth because we are told that he lived like a hermit and dressed in animal skins, eating locusts and wild honey. It may well have been that he had lived with the well-established community of the Essenes, who lived in the hills above the Dead Sea and some of whose documents, hidden no doubt at the time of the destruction of Jerusalem and discovered almost one hundred years ago, revealed their deeply Jewish roots. In his preaching, he made it quite clear that he was the prophetic voice crying in the wilderness, "Prepare the way of the Lord." And much of his knowledge of the Jewish scriptures may have come from the Essenes.

However, John's role was twofold. He announced that the Kingdom of God was very near, and he identified Jesus as the one who would inaugurate it. When Jesus came to be baptized by him in the Jordan, John announced to the crowd that this was God's appointed one, saying of Him, "Behold the Lamb of God." He also testified that he had seen the Holy Spirit descend on Jesus and stay there. John then said that God had told him to baptize with water and that when he saw the Holy Spirit descend and remain on a man, He was to declare that He was the one who was to follow him. John then said, "I have seen it, and I tell you, He is the Son of God."

Jesus As God Incarnate

As soon as one begins to look at the New Testament, one immediately becomes aware that one character dominates the whole of the series of books of which it is composed. That person is, of course, Jesus of Nazareth, who, it was claimed, was the Son of God. However, His human life on earth is a total enigma. He was born to an undistinguished family in the north of the country, and his first 30 years of existence appear to have been so completely in character with his family and neighbours. He was apparently seen by everyone just as the eldest son of a working-class family. Even in His local synagogue it appears that He was undistinguished, hence the statement recorded in Luke 4:22. When Jesus stood up to read from the scripture, the people's comment was, "Is not this Joseph the carpenter's son?"

And yet his birth had been spectacularly different. A birth announced by angels to a young girl engaged to be married to the village carpenter, who, when he discovered that the girl in question was pregnant, married her to spare her embarrassment, because he was told, again by angelic messengers, that his wife-to-be had not been unfaithful but was to carry a special child, chosen by God to be the long-expected Messiah and born of God's Spirit. The birth, when it happened, at the end of a tiring journey from Nazareth to Bethlehem to register for the census, was perfectly normal except that some shepherds keeping watch over their sheep in the summer pasture had seen a mighty vision – of an angelic choir who sang and an angel who told them that a child had been born in a local stable, a child who was to be their king. They then rushed off to see whether it was true and startled the parents of this newborn baby by telling them about the amazing vision which they had just seen. Then it was life as usual for the family until some two years later they had a most extraordinary visit from some foreign astrologers, who brought lavish gifts because, they said, they had seen the indication in the stars that this child was destined to be the future king of Israel. But the child in question appears to have shown no indication of either His status or His enormous potential, although Mary in particular had stored these facts in her mind. But we must remember, this all happened in Bethlehem, many miles distant from the province of Galilee, where they went to live after returning from Egypt, where they had been sent, again by God's warning, to escape from the malicious slaughter of all male children of two years of age or under, which had been Herod's reaction to the astrologers' news that a baby had been born who would become the King of the Jews. An action reminiscent of Pharaoh's attempt to reduce the Israelite population in Egypt by ordering the death of all baby boys.

If we look at Jesus' parents for some clues to His identity, we find little about their background to explain the events which would follow. By contrast, John the Baptist's parents were both members of the priestly Levitical tribe. Both were elderly, long past childbearing and childless. Both are named and their parentage is noted. Zechariah was a priest of the clan of Abia, and his wife, Elizabeth, was of the daughters of Aaron, and her name was Elizabeth (Luke 1:5). We are told that they were godly and disciplined in character, and Zechariah was performing his appointed duties in the Temple when an angel appeared to him to say that his prayer for a child would be answered: Though it seems strange that a man of his age would be praying for a child. In the case of John, it may well have been either that Elizabeth, like Hannah, Samuel's mother, and like Rachel, Jacob's wife, was desperate for a child, feeling that for a woman not to bear a child was to deny her primary function as a woman. Whilst for a man the desire for a child was most often the desire to continue his family line. What we do know is that Zechariah was told that his son would be a person of significance: "He shall be great in the sight of the Lord… He shall be filled with the Holy Spirit even from his mother's womb." Because Zechariah questioned the angel's words, finding it difficult to believe, as he said, that at their age he and his wife could have a child, he was struck dumb. Not to regain the power of speech until the child was born. At which point the Holy Spirit came on him, and he prophesied in challenging words, saying that they were about to experience a visitation from God, the fulfilment of what the prophets of old had forecast. Luke 1:67–79. We are then told that the child grew in strength and spirit and was in the deserts "till the day of his showing unto Israel." We know that John's function was to 'prepare the way of the Lord', which he did by declaring that the prophetic vision was about to be fulfilled, making converts, and then baptizing them in the Jordan, which was an innovation which would be continued by the disciples of Jesus. What is interesting is that at a time of rebellion and unrest under Roman rule, John attracted a considerable number of followers, some of whom were priests.

Because John's parents were elderly when he was born, it is quite likely that he spent his early years with a known group of aesthetics known as the Essenes, who lived in the desert places above the Dead Sea and not far from Jerusalem and whose collection of writings was apparently hidden during the time of the destruction of the city in AD 70 and which was discovered by shepherd lads in the early part of this last century. When, finally, they were pieced together and able to be deciphered, they were found to contain scrolls of Old Testament writings, some from Isaiah. Those scrolls are still being examined and are known as the Dead Sea scrolls because they were found hidden in the caves in the rocks about the Dead Sea.

In the sixth month of Elizabeth's pregnancy, an angel was sent to a city in the northern district of Galilee called Nazareth. The young girl chosen to be the mother of Jesus, Mary, is simply referred to by Luke in his gospel as "a virgin espoused to a man whose name was Joseph of the house of David." Luke 1:27. Whilst we know a great deal about what the angel told her – that she had found favour with God and that the child she would bear would be called "the Son of the Highest," that His name should be Jesus, and that "the Lord God shall give unto Him the throne of His father David." Of her parentage, we know little, only that she appears to have been related to Elizabeth, John's mother.

Mary was obviously both startled and disturbed, because although she was 'espoused' to be married, she was not married. However, she would have known that her 'espoused' husband was 'of the house of David', so, although this idea that the child would be born of the Holy Spirit as the Son of God was effectively beyond her understanding, the concept of her son being a king, through her marriage to Joseph, was something which would possibly help her to understand the significance of the later visit of the Magi.

Mary's immediate response was to visit her cousin Elizabeth because, in confirmation of what he had said, the angel told her that Elizabeth was six months pregnant in her old age. Mary's response to the angel's message was that of one who had a firm faith in God, for she did not query anything but merely said, "Be it unto me according to thy word." Then she 'arose with haste' and travelled from Nazareth down south to the hills above Judea to visit this cousin, Elizabeth, and she stayed there for about three months. What transpired between those two women is recorded for us by Luke, verses 39–55, and it was a very deeply moving experience of the power of the Holy Spirit in speaking to them. All of which would have been valuable and helpful to both, but especially to Mary, because she was so young, probably only about 14 to 15 years of age. Girls of that age were frequently 'espoused' in marriage to older men who had the means and the ability to support a wife and family.

Of Joseph, we know little, except that he was a carpenter and that he was born into the tribe of Judah, which was the royal lineage of their famous king David. However, from his response to the news and his actions afterwards, he was obviously a good and loving man who knew God and was prepared to accept his role. As soon as he became aware of the situation, whether from Mary herself or the angel, as is most likely from Matthew 1:20, he decided to treat the matter privately. In other words, not to embarrass Mary publicly, and then he was quick to respond positively to the instruction from an angel to marry her despite the obvious problem. There was no criticism, although the situation in which he was placed would have presented major problems for most men.

Obviously older than Mary, Joseph would have waited until he was well established before considering marriage, and therefore, he would have been better placed to face the very substantial financial burden placed on him. First, the issue of having to travel to register in his family home of Bethlehem with Mary, a considerable journey for a pregnant woman close to birth, and then the issue of providing for his family. We know that the family stayed on in Bethlehem for some two years because, from the dates given to Herod by the 'wise men', the birth had been some time earlier. The idea of the wise men arriving at the cattle shed is romantic but clearly untrue; by that time, the family was living in a house.

Then the journey into Egypt! This is probably less arduous than it seems because we know that there was a Jewish community living in Northeastern Egypt, in the Nile delta, probably close to their original settlement in Goshen, so he would have had help and, potentially, employment until he was told to return. Once again, a problem! There are conflicting accounts here. According to Matthew, Joseph was told by an angel in a dream to return home, but Judea was not safe because the new ruler, following Herod's death, was his son Archelaus. So, Joseph took his new family to the province of Galilee and made his home in Nazareth, which, in those days, was a substantial, populous city. Luke gives us a different account. He ignores the visit of the wise men and the subsequent threat to the young children born at that time. Luke tells us that to fulfil the Jewish law at eight days, his parents took the baby to the Temple in Jerusalem to be circumcised and then returned 'to their hometown in Nazareth'. Luke 2:39. Obviously the details of our Lord's early life were not seen as specifically relevant, merely that those details should comply with the prophecies concerning Him, which would validate what the disciples would teach about His royal lineage.

These two separate accounts from different writers suggest that these writers had different sources. What we do know is that right from the start of Mary's pregnancy, the whole matter required, indeed depended on, the total cooperation of ordinary human beings, who were being led and guided by the Holy Spirit. In the same way that any fully committed and surrendered Christian can be led and guided in their life, although not necessarily with such dramatic results.

The only recorded incident in the childhood of Jesus, which might have given a clue to His future spectacular ministry, occurred when He was 12 years old, during the family's annual visit from their home in Nazareth to the Temple in Jerusalem. The festival over, the family group had started on the laborious journey home, a large group by all accounts, and Jesus, aged 12 and the eldest of seven children, was understood to have been with His siblings, like any other responsible boy of his age. It was only late in the day when His parents found that he was not in the group. Most parents will have had some incident of this kind when a child is not where he or she should be and the anxiety involved.

However, there was now serious concern when a search through the group failed to locate Him. The parents then left the group and their other children and returned to Jerusalem to search for him. They searched for three days, obviously revisiting the places in which they had stayed and the most likely places to interest a child of that age. Three days of great anxiety searching before they finally found Him in the Temple, calmly discussing with the doctors of the Law, both listening and asking questions. When challenged by His parents, who, by this time, must have been distraught, He simply answered, "Didn't you understand that I must be about My Father's business?" This statement is an indication that Jesus Himself knew who he was and that He was on earth for a purpose, to serve God, His true father, not to become a carpenter like His 'assumed' father, Joseph. The fact that His parents did not understand what He meant clearly shows how 'out of character' this event was. Suggesting to us that His childhood was that of an ordinary child. It is also interesting that of the four Gospel writers, only Luke mentions this incident, possibly because his account gives us the greatest amount of information about His early years. We know that he was a doctor, and his account of Paul's life reveals a close record of details.

Remarkably, it was only after achieving manhood, at the age of thirty that his unique character and actions marked him out as someone unusual, although His Mother's words to Him at the marriage in Cana suggest that she knew or expected something. To all others He was nothing more than a normal child, so much so that He was described by his neighbours, on that moment when He read the scriptures in His local synagogue in Nazareth, simply as 'Jesus of Nazareth, the carpenter's son'. Yet, every other character in the book and all the subsequent events are related in some way to the person who was described later by the Roman historian Tacitus as having been "executed by Pontius Pilate, the Roman governor of the province." And the reason that he made that comment was that His coming, His birth to a humble family, and His subsequent death at the hands of the Romans would change the whole course of the world's history. The life of Jesus of Nazareth would in itself have been a seven-day wonder, soon forgotten, had it not been that someone, other than His immediate disciples, was also aware that His death was significant. How much more would have been written had the writer known or believed that after three days Jesus came alive, would be seen by upwards of 500 people, and then disappear back into the heavens after promising to return? No one at that point could have known that these events would have an enormous impact on future world events, greater than any other figure in the whole history of civilization, and that two thousand years later, millions of people would still celebrate both His birth and His death. What an achievement for barely three years of work. And the reason His life had such an enormous effect was that this man, Jesus, was Almighty God become incarnate.

The almost unbelievable recognition that the invisible God, the creator of the Universe, had chosen to make Himself known to His creation by taking the form of one of His created beings and experiencing life just like the rest of us was too wonderful for humanity to accept it or act upon it. Except for a small number of ordinary people, whose witness through the following ages of time has perpetuated and kept alive the miracle of it all in the form of our Christian religion, and they, those who truly believe these facts, are the true 'children of God'.

The reference by Tacitus, which I have mentioned, is the only known written reference, by historians of the time, to the existence of this Jesus, whose life and teaching would come to underwrite the whole of Western civilization. During his lifetime and in the years following his martyrdom, his own followers had no motive for recording his life and teaching, and there is a specific reason for this. The reason was that three days after his cruel death at the hands of the Roman authorities, he was seen to be alive. Seen, in fact, as we are later told, by over 500 people and seen for some 40 days before he disappeared from their sight. However, what inhibited any contemporary written records was the statement he made before his death that, following his resurrection to life and having been seen alive by many people, He would disappear from human sight and return to the Heaven from which He had come. Therefore, His disciples had been told that this was what to expect. It was nothing new. And they had been told that He would soon reappear physically before the whole world at the head of a great company of angels. All of which was later recorded for posterity by all four Gospel writers. Matthew in his chapter 24:3 ff, Luke in his chapter 21:20 ff, Mark 13:3 ff, and John 14:3. And they also recorded the cataclysmic events which He had foretold would happen during the lifetime of his followers. Presumably, what happened in AD 70. Therefore, there was no need to make any record of his life, because they were totally convinced that it would shortly become self-evident on His return. Paul himself shared this view, that the return of Jesus was imminent, and states it in his writings. As does James in his letter, chapter 5:8:

It was only after some thirty or more years had passed since His resurrection and ascension into heaven without any sign of his reappearance that any thought of recording those events was even considered necessary. At first, the disciples believed that our Lord's return to earth was imminent, and they frequently say that. Further, during this time the rebellious nation, under the guidance of the leading family, the Maccabees, rebelled against the Roman rule to such an extent that the Roman Emperor Vespasian had ordered the destruction of the capital city, Jerusalem, together with its Temple, and the exile of all its inhabitants. Only then was it understood that the need for a written record became imperative. As Luke himself points out at the beginning of his written record, Luke 1:1–4. Not least because a new generation was emerging that had either not been alive at the time or whose need for a more permanent record to be made became important. And this was also a consequence of the destruction of their Temple in Jerusalem, which had been a focus for the nation's Jewish ancestry and heritage. From that time until now, for Jews, the focus is on 'The Book', the written word of God's Covenant and His Law. What we must understand is that the account which we find in the 27 books of the New Testament is fully in accord with what we later find developing as the Christian narrative, which became the basis of all Christian belief and was formulated for us as what we know as the 'Creed'. This was the document, based on selected books that were recognized as having a divine origin, which was assembled at the conference held at Nicaea in 325 AD, under the auspices of the Emperor Constantine, who had 'converted' to the Christian faith. And it is this document which has formed the basis of belief for all Western Christianity, whether Roman Catholic, Anglican, or other nonconformist Protestant churches, and it is this core of belief holds the whole Christian community together.

Chapter 2
The Written Record

What we now know as the Christian Bible is in two parts. The Old Testament was originally written mostly in Hebrew, with some Aramaic in the later parts of Isaiah, Jeremiah, and Ezra. Hebrew being the Jewish language whilst Aramaic was the general language of West Euphrates. The New Testament was then written in Greek, which had become the universal language of the educated world and was a valuable aid in the spread of early Christianity, as was the facilitation of transport introduced by the construction and safeguarding of roads by the Romans.

What we must understand is that the material of the Bible was given by God by inspiration, not as a complete record but as an unfolding revelation. So what God told the Old Testament patriarchs, like Abraham, was nowhere as complex as what He revealed to men like Paul. Right from the beginning in Genesis, we have an unfolding, developing revelation of God to us, but much of it, as in the lives of Adam, Abraham, and Moses, can be seen in the symbolic images, which only became understood as the narrative progressed.

Remember that Jesus had told His disciples that after He returned to His Father, God, His Father would give them the gift of the Holy Spirit. And that Holy Spirit would "lead them into all truth." John 14:17 and John 16:12. What we have today was compiled from various manuscripts. The earliest version of the complete Old Testament is probably the Septuagint version, written in Greek, which originated around 285 B.C. and was produced by the Jewish people. Its name derives from the 70 translators who composed it. However, probably the best-known version of the whole Bible is St Jerome's Latin version, 385/404 AD, called the Vulgate, meaning a 'common' or readily understood text. And this remained for many years the formative text of the Church for some 1,000 years. But, with the decline of Latin as a universal language over the centuries, the Bible was lost to the common people and remained as a text for the educated scholars and educated priests.

The beginning of a new age in Christian history begins with the production of a version in the language of the laity. A version which could be read and understood by ordinary people. This was first produced as a translation by the reformer Wycliffe, the first part of which appeared in 1380 and was completed before he died in 1384. However, the weakness of this was that Wycliffe had simply translated Jerome's Vulgate from Latin into the English of his day; there was no attempt to resource the original Hebrew or the original Greek versions.

The next innovation was really brought about at the end of the Fifteenth Century by what we call the Renaissance. The rediscovery of the old Greek language and of original texts. Martin Luther helped in this by his translation, probably from prison, which he completed in German in 1534. However, Wycliffe's language, some two hundred years earlier, was archaic and not easily understood by this time, so the appearance of a new version by Tyndale was a great step forward for two reasons. First, he went back to the original sources, in Greek and Hebrew, but secondly, he wrote so that 'a ploughboy could understand as readily as an educated churchman'. And this first appeared in 1530. This was then followed by a number of other versions, mostly based on Tyndale, such as Miles Coverdale's translation in 1535, Cranmer's or the Great Bible in 1539, and the Geneva Bible in 1560. Finally, it was from Tyndale's translation that, in 1610, would come the version that is still in use today, the 'Authorised Version', which was motivated by the Puritans and sanctioned by the King, James 1st, which had been translated and most carefully researched by 47 men appointed by the King.

Today we have several 'modern' versions, including The New English Bible, The Revised Standard Bible, and more recently The Good News Bible, with intermediate versions by Moffat and Weymouth and J.B. Phillips version of the Epistles. What we have to remember is two things: first, that the earliest 'believers' saw no need to record the events of Jesus' life because they all believed that His return was imminent; therefore, there was no need to attempt to make any permanent record; and, secondly, that with the destruction of the city and its Temple by the Romans in AD 70 and the subsequent exile of its inhabitants, the native Jewish Christian community soon died out or was dispersed, and the main focus, as recorded in The Acts of the Apostles and in the Epistles, was directed to Greek-speaking peoples who were scattered throughout

Asia Minor. Introduced largely because of the preaching of the converted Jewish Pharisee, Paul, who had been born in the Roman province of Tarsus in the Greek-speaking Roman province of Cilicia. He was a Hebrew scholar, educated as a strict Pharisee in Jerusalem, where he lived with his sister.

A good thing about this destruction of the Jewish Temple, the city, and the nation was that what might have ended as another Jewish sect rapidly became an international religion, carried by the exiles, and which would encompass all the then-known world. Most of which was part of the expanding Roman Empire and in which, following the earlier conquests of the Greeks under Alexander the Great, had become largely Greek-speaking. Because Greek had become the language of educated society. Greek was the language of the poets and dramatists, such as Euripides, Aeschylus, and Pindar, and of course Homer, and of the philosophers such as Plato and Aristotle. In fact, it has been said that it was the security of the Roman Empire with its laws, its roads, and military discipline, combined with the universal use of the Greek language, which facilitated the rapid growth and expansion of Christianity for many centuries. Perhaps the most important event was the conversion of the Roman emperor Constantine to the Christian faith. Exactly how or when this happened is not known. Some say he was influenced by his mother, Helen, but others say it was a vision of the Cross which he saw before his great victory at the Battle of Milvian Bridge in 312 AD against his chief rival, Maxentius, which he attributed to a belief in Christ. Following his vision, he had ordered his soldiers to paint the cross on their shields. However, we do know that as early as 307, he began favouring the position of Christians in the Empire, reversing the earlier Roman persecution of the followers of Christ. Soon he was to make Christianity the official faith of the Empire. A move which many saw as political rather than religious because, at this time, Rome was beginning to suffer from opposing forces and from internal conflict over leadership, and he saw the rapid advance of the new faith as a means of strengthening the position of Rome throughout Europe and into Asia. In fact, the great 6th-century edifice we know as St Sophia, which was built by the Emperor Justinian, was built on the site of an earlier church built by Constantine in 325.

Before we go any further, I want us to consider the four persons whose names are attributed as being the writers of the four Gospels, which have become the record of the life and ministry of Jesus. We have no certain record that the Gospels were written by these men, but traditionally, and with reason, we have accepted their authorship. They are important because they are the only authentic record of our Lord's life. The first three are known as synonymous gospels because they appear to share similar accounts and a similar order, possibly similar source material, although they differ in many respects, most notably in their opening chapters.

Matthew begins with the genealogy of Jesus through his adoptive 'father' Joseph, tracing his ancestry from Abraham through the royal tribe of Judah. Mark, by contrast, begins with the ministry of His cousin John the Baptist and the baptism of Jesus, which began the period of His ministry. Luke, however, whom we recognize as Paul's beloved physician, begins with all the details of the background, John's birth to the elderly Zechariah and Elizabeth, both from the priestly tribe. Then we have the only record of Mary's experience with the angelic messenger six months later and Joseph's response, followed by the journey to Bethlehem and again the only record of the actual birth of Jesus. All of this is written in considerable detail, occupying some three chapters leading up to the start of our Lord's ministry and His temptation in chapter 4. Luke also gives us an account of our Lord's ancestry, but in this case going back to Seth, the son of Adam.

However, the Gospel as written by John takes a very different route, taking us back to the creation and acknowledging our Lord's presence there. "In the beginning the Word already existed; the Word was with God, and the Word was God." Before introducing John the Baptist and his recognition of Jesus as "the Lamb of God who takes away the sin of the world." Which is a very startling statement and implies that John, of all the disciples, had a closer bond with Jesus and hence a more intimate understanding of who and what He was. Which is subsequently confirmed by subtle detail in the text itself, suggesting that either he understood more or was told more than the other disciples. John is also referred to as 'the disciple whom Jesus loved'.

Matthew

Matthew the disciple may not have been the Matthew who wrote the gospel; there is nothing in scripture to make the connection. What we do know of the call of Matthew the disciple is that he was a tax collector, also called a publican, as mentioned in the gospel of Matthew, chapter 9:9. Mark also mentions the same incident in Mark 2:14, and Luke adds that after his call he gave a great feast to which other publicans, tax collectors, etc. were invited (Luke 5:27). So he was

148

most likely to have been one of the early disciples of Jesus, a tax collector, at whose house Jesus was entertained. However, if this disciple is the same as Matthew, the writer of the Gospel, it would explain his intimate knowledge of the events of Jesus' life, but we would also expect him to have had a greater knowledge of the more intimate moments, as we find, for example, in John's account, had he been with Jesus during his years of ministry.

Mark

The second writer is named Mark, and this is where the puzzle begins, because he is not named as a disciple. However, do not despair because we are certain that we do know who he is. It would appear from the latter text that he is John Mark, the son of Mary Mark, who was one of those who entertained Jesus and the disciples at her home in Jerusalem. And this house may have been the house of the Upper Room where the Last Supper was held. We are told that the house to which Peter went, when released from prison, and at which Rhoda the servant girl was so excited to hear his voice that she forgot to let him in, belonged to "Mary the mother of John whose surname was Mark." Acts 12:12. This being the case, then this Mark is, very likely, the young man who fled from the arrest of Jesus in the Garden, leaving his outer garment behind. Mark 14:51. This is most likely to be so because Mark is the only one who mentions the incident in his Gospel. This John Mark reappears later as the one who accompanied Paul and Barnabas on their first missionary journey (Acts 13:5) but who left them at Pamphylia and returned home to Jerusalem. However, when Paul and Barnabas set off on the second journey, Barnabas wanted to take John Mark with them, possibly because he was his cousin (Colossians 4:19), but Paul was not happy about taking him because he had left them at Pamphylia and returned home. This led to a major dispute, with the result that Paul took Silas with him and Barnabas took John Mark. Acts 15:36–40. This dispute between these two men would make it likely that Barnabus was related to Mary Mark, the mother of this John Mark. We do know that Barnabus was a leading figure amongst the Jerusalem Christians and that he was the one who went to Tarsus to fetch the converted Saul of Tarsus, later named Paul, and who accompanied Paul on his first missionary journey. We then find further reference to Mark as a companion of Paul during his imprisonment in Rome, Colossians 4:11, where he is also referred to as "a much desired fellow worker" during Paul's second period in prison, 2 Timothy 4:11. And he is also referred to by Peter as 'My son', 1 Peter

5:13. Knowing Peter's friendship with Mark's mother, it might well be that it was Peter who introduced him to Jesus as a convert. In which case the young Mark would have had ample opportunity to become acquainted with the details of our Lord's life, probably added to by Peter.

Luke

The identity of Luke is less of a problem because, although he was not mentioned as one of the early disciples, he claims to have an intimate knowledge of the facts, Luke 1:1–4. We know that he was the physician who joined Paul on his missionary journey, Acts 16:10. We can deduce this simply because up until the previous verse, Paul was referred to in the third person, 'he', but after this, the pronoun used is 'we', implying that at this point, Luke had joined the party, which accounts for the very detailed description of Paul's final journey to Rome, and we know that he was with him there in prison. Which is confirmed later from Paul's own testimony when he refers to him as "our beloved doctor." Colossians 4:14, and that is also confirmed in Philemon 24, where he is named with Demas and mentioned in Paul's second letter to Timothy 4:11 as being with him in prison. We also know that he was the author of the Acts of the Apostles and that he wrote the Gospel of his name because he says so. Acts 1:1. His time with Paul, listening to his preaching, etc. would have given him the knowledge which he had missed by not being a disciple. In later life, he appears, as he says in Acts 1:2–3, to have been the instructor or teacher of a boy who was the son of someone of considerable consequence. The mystery is, what happened to Paul, who was in prison in Rome?

John

John, the fourth writer, is most easily identified from his intimate knowledge of who Jesus really was, as expressed in his first chapter verses 1–5 and is known as the disciple closest to Jesus, John 13:23. Matthew 20:20 refers to the strange request of the mother of James and John, asking for preferment in the Kingdom for her two sons, so she believed that there was a special closeness. Like his brother James, he had been a fisherman, and we first meet him when Jesus called the first four of his disciples by the lake Galilee. Matthew 4:21. He and his brother, sons of Zebedee, appear to have had connections with the priesthood because at the arrest, when Jesus was taken into the High Priest's house, we are told that one of the disciples, John (18:15), had access because he was known to

150

the High Priest, and it is only John who mentions this. If this status was correct, it could also account for John's mother's request for her two sons, James and John, to have the chief positions in our Lord's kingdom. John's Gospel contains some of the most intimate details of our Lord's relationship with His Father, as he records the words of Jesus' prayer and in his disclosures of some intimate details of Jesus life, especially in the closing days, as in chapters 14, 15, and 16, which suggest an intimacy which was unique amongst the disciples. It also accounts for His words in John 19:27 when Jesus commits the care of His mother to John. But all this does not exclude our Lord's criticism of James and John after their mother's request (Matthew 20:22).

It is interesting also that where the first three Gospels appear to rely on combined or commonly known facts, with even their chronology being similar, John's account stands alone, with detail not recorded by the first three, and John was the author of three letters to the Church and the remarkable visions revealed in the book of Revelation, which we find very difficult to understand, but the symbolism of which, most probably, would have been understood by the churches to whom it was sent. One major source of confusion is the fact that whilst it comprises a series of visions, these visions are not in chronological order. So, we cannot ask, "Where are we now in this ongoing saga?"

So, we know that the life of Jesus and the account of His birth, His ancestry and His public ministry from the age of 30, and the events which ultimately ended with His death were not put on record until some years after His resurrection and ascent into heaven. Further, the disciples would also, by that time, have had the benefit of the coming of the Holy Spirit who, as Jesus had promised, would "lead them into all truth" (John 16:13).

Chapter 3
The Main Actors

The twelve Apostles

Of the twelve disciples called as apostles of the faith, four immediately stand out. They are the four fishermen from Lake Galilee. Jesus called them as he walked along the shores of the lake, and Matthew says that this is where Jesus first met Simon (whom he called Peter), Andrew his brother, and their partners, James and John the sons of Zebedee. However, John in his Gospel, 1:37–40, says that Andrew was a disciple of John the Baptist and that he heard John point Jesus out as the 'Lamb of God' and that he went and met Jesus and then found his brother Simon (whom Jesus renamed Peter) and introduced him to Jesus. Of these, Peter would always be the most outspoken, the impetuous one who was the first to acknowledge that Jesus was the Messiah, but he was also the first to deny that he knew Jesus during that awful night in the house of Annas the High Priest, following the arrest in the garden. John 18:15. Jesus, anticipating this, had predicted it and promised to pray for him. Luke 22:31. This incident, related by John, also implies, by not naming him, that he, John, was the one who was well known to the High Priest. There are several suggestions in the text that Zebedee's family were well born, not least their mother's request that her two sons be given senior positions in Jesus' government when He became king. What we do know is that John was the disciple closest to Jesus and that he is described as "the one whom Jesus loved." However, the three most often named as being close to Jesus were Peter, James and John. For example, they were the three disciples whom Jesus took with Him up the mountain where He would be 'transfigured'. They would also hear His Father say, "This is my beloved Son, in whom I am well pleased." And see Him speaking with Moses and Elijah, who had died so many years earlier.

Matthew himself tells us that he was a 'tax collector' whom Jesus called (Matthew 9:9), and John tells us in Chapter 1:43 that Jesus first met Philip and called him on His way to Galilee, and that Philip then found Nathaniel and told him that Jesus was the one about whom the prophets had spoken and then introduced him to Jesus. Of Philip, little is known, but John tells us that he was from Bethsaida, the home of Peter and Andrew, which suggests that they knew each other. In this account Jesus questions Nathaniel's belief, calling him a true Israelite 'in whom was no guile'. Nathaniel accepted our Lord's authenticity because He was able to say that He had 'seen him under the fig tree', implying that Jesus had an unusual ability. These details are interesting because they shed some light on the background, the how and why of our Lord's choice of men to be with Him. Which also, for example, indicates that He would have known all about Judas, right from the moment he joined the group.

This then accounts for seven of the Apostles of the early days. Of the other five, we have no record at this point. Although, again by John's implication, they were all possibly present at the wedding in Cana of Galilee when Jesus performed His first miracle by turning a vast quantity of water into wine. We do, however, have a record of their names as being the men Jesus chose and sent out to preach the good news, and that list, provided by Matthew, Mark, and Luke but not John, adds Thomas, James the son of Alphaeus, Thaddeus, Simon the Patriot, and Judas Iscariot, who betrayed Him. The other interesting thing about these five is that Thomas is only really mentioned twice in the text, and then most notably for his difficulty in believing that Jesus was alive after the resurrection. He was not with the other ten when Jesus appeared to them, and he had said that he would only believe if he could actually see our Lord's wounds. John tells us that a week later Jesus appeared when Thomas was there, and Thomas was only then convinced. John 20:24–29. The only other apostle mentioned later was, of course, Judas, who betrayed Him, and apart from that, all we only know of him was that he kept the common purse and had been helping himself to the money. After his betrayal of Jesus, Judas, presumably out of remorse, committed suicide. We often wonder what drove him to that fatal action of betrayal. Was it for the money, or was it because he wanted to force Jesus to act, to declare Himself King? We shall never know because scripture is silent. After Judas' death, out of the two proposed candidates, Mattias was chosen because he had been with them from the beginning, but once again we hear no more of him.

The Disciples

Apart from the twelve, several other men are mentioned in relation to specific events. These include Nicodemus, a leading Pharisee who came to Jesus by night, asking for further details of our Lord's message, John 3:16. He had joined Joseph, a rich disciple from Arimathea and a well-respected member of the Council who was waiting for the Kingdom of God, in begging our Lord's body from Pilate and burying it in his newly excavated tomb. Once again, it is only John who records this and the fact that Nicodemus brought some 30 kilos of spices to anoint the body. John 19:39. It is obvious that there were several hidden 'disciples', men and women, who believed but were unwilling to openly align themselves with Jesus in those early days. Two others, not previously named but who were obviously totally committed, are Cleopas and a friend whom Jesus took the trouble to meet on their journey to Emmaus on that day, and He listened to their description of their sad news, their personal record of what they believed had happened, before revealing Himself to them as they sat at a meal. We then see them, deeply impressed, rushing all the way back to Jerusalem, late at night, to share the news with the other disciples, who at first did not believe them. It is interesting to note that all the other witnesses of the resurrected Christ confirm that the Apostles themselves had great difficulty in accepting that Jesus was alive and visibly present with them. The various messages from the first people to see Him, such as Mary and the women, had confused them. It was only after they had seen and spoken to Him themselves that they were fully convinced. Whereas, had the official version been true, that the disciples had stolen the body and manufactured the idea of His resurrection, then surely they, the Apostles, would have been the first ones to tell everyone.

Had the accusation, fabricated by the authorities in an attempt to mislead the public, been true, that the disciples had stolen the body to foster the idea that He was still alive, then the idea that He was alive would have originated with the disciples themselves, trying to convince others. That the reverse is true, that the ones closest to Jesus found it most difficult to believe, makes the evidence more convincing. The resurrection was a truly supernatural event, which not only supported His claim to be the eternal Son of God, who had come to earth for a very limited period, only to return to His Father when His work on earth was complete. It was and is the evidence of life after death for all believers. As Paul later said, "If in this life only we have hope in Christ, we are of all men most miserable." 1 Corinthians 15:18. It is well worth reading the whole of the passage about the resurrection of Christ and its meaning for us.

The story gathers pace as we hear of the seven deacons chosen to assist in the daily administration, including Stephen, whose ministry was so powerful in the Holy Spirit that he was taken outside the city and stoned to death, and that is where we first meet Saul of Tarsus. Philip was most likely to have been the one to convince the Ethiopian Eunuch, an important official from Ethiopia who was a converted Jew returning from worship in Jerusalem and reading from the book of Isaiah. He was puzzled over who Isaiah was referring to in describing the 'suffering servant' of Isaiah 53. The account of their meeting is described in Acts 8:26ff. Philip had also been mightily used by God in bringing the Gospel to Samaria, Acts 8:4. Of the others, Prochorus, Nicanor, Timon, Parmenas, and Nicholaus, a Jewish convert, we hear nothing more, but the success of their work is obvious in the rapid growth in number of the converts, as the news of Jesus was taken to the areas surrounding Jerusalem. On the other hand, Ananias and Sapphira achieved a measure of fame solely because of their attempt to deceive the Apostles by lying about the value of their land. As Peter said, before they sold it, it was theirs, but to sell it and then lie about its value was to attempt to deceive, to receive praise without paying the price.

The Role Of The Women

The importance of the women who followed Jesus is often overlooked. As is frequently the case today, people recognise the leading figures but ignore the 'behind the scenes' work, without which the men up front could not operate. First of these is obviously Mary, who gave birth to Jesus and brought Him up only to see the words of the prophet Simeon to Mary in the Temple at the ceremony of purification fulfilled. Luke 2:35 "And sorrow like a sword shall break your own heart." Certainly, Mary was present at the Cross and saw Him die. With her, John tells us were Mary's sister, Mary the wife of Clopas and Mary Magdalene. Mary Magdalene was the Mary in the garden weeping at the tomb, to whom Jesus spoke after she had mistaken Him for the gardener; He was so altered by His suffering. It is believed that this Mary, for whom Jesus had done so much, was genuinely and romantically in love with Him, but Jesus would not have entered an exclusive relationship with any one individual; He belongs to all believers. Also, because, as God's Son, He was a spiritual being who, within days, would

155

be back in Heaven, where she could not go. Ultimately, all of God's children, as heirs together with Christ, will be with Him forever in an eternal existence.

Then there were people like Mary and Martha, the sisters of Jesus' friend Lazarus, who entertained Jesus. And Zebedee's wife who asked that her sons, James and John, should have senior positions in the Kingdom. The Samaritan woman at the well of Sychar, the Canaanite woman who begged successfully for her daughter's healing, the widow of Nain, whose son Jesus raised to life, and the woman with an 'issue of blood', who was healed by touching His robe. But above all these, seen and unseen, were many women who followed Him as disciples and 'ministered' to Him. Caring, no doubt, for His personal needs as He travelled the country.

Paul The Apostle

Once we move beyond the Gospels, the dominant figure through the whole of the New Testament is Saul of Tarsus, later called Paul. Paul was in fact a considerable figure and one with what he believed was an assured future before he so dramatically met Jesus as he travelled to Damascus and was converted to the new Christian faith, whose followers he had been persecuting. He was born in Tarsus, which, because it was a Roman city, gave him the benefit of Roman citizenship as well as his Hebrew ancestry, which he inherited from his parents. He had been sent to Jerusalem to study under Gamaliel, a leading Jewish leader. He belonged to the strictest of the religious groups, the Pharisees, who dominated the religious observance of the city of Jerusalem. They believed in the strictest observance of Hebrew law, accepted without question the authority of the Law, the Torah, and he was clearly extremely zealous and active within that sect because he sought and obtained authority from the leaders of their religion to seek out and to imprison, even to kill, the followers of 'The Way'. Because he believed that this new 'sect', as it was believed to be, was undermining their own Jewish beliefs and that Jesus, by His very open criticism of the Pharisees, was challenging their authority. What Jesus taught was seen by the Pharisees as both a deviant sect and a danger to the spiritual welfare of the nation. Paul's zeal would have been driven by an absolute hatred of this upstart, Jesus, whose disciples were disturbing the authority of his leaders and threatening their position under their Roman overlords. His disciples even asserted that Jesus was not dead but had been raised to life by God Himself. It was the High Priest who had said, when advocating sending Jesus to be put to death by the Roman authorities, "Better this one man perish than the whole nation be in jeopardy." So, Paul had the moral and religious support of his superiors when he began his rigorous seeking out of the followers of this Jesus.

What is so notable is that after his 'conversion' on the road to Damascus, which led to his rejection of his Pharisaical background and his espousal of the 'Jesus' cause, he would be persecuted and imprisoned by those very people whose beliefs he had originally promoted. His total commitment to the cause of Christ and the enormous suffering he endured because of it must have been very apparent when he said, "If in this life only we have hope in Christ, we are of all men most miserable." 1 Corinthians 15:19.

Serving as a Pharisee had obvious benefits. Prestige, wealth and a high position in society. All of which Paul had sacrificed to become a follower of Jesus, and his reward in life then became suffering, pain, beatings, imprisonment and finally, death. So, if human life was everything and the future bleak, then Christianity was not worth the risk. Better to stay as a Jew and look for their reward in paradise. But no! Paul believed that the future was so wonderful that all the pain and problems seemed as nothing compared to the joy and bliss of eternity as a child of God. Paul wrote similar words about the suffering endured by Jesus. "Who for the joy set before Him endured the cross, despising the shame, and is seated now at the right hand of the Father." Hebrews 12:2

With his education, especially his understanding of the Hebraic language and its law, and his fluency in the Greek language, Paul was the ideal person intellectually and, from his personal encounter with Jesus on the road to Damascus, spiritually, to see that the work of Christ was the literal fulfilment of the Old Testament and its symbolism. He was able to link the two and understand that it was not some new religion foisted upon humanity but that the Christian faith was the continuation of the work which God had begun with Adam and had concluded in Christ Jesus. Further, as a human being, his total dedication and commitment, his compassion and understanding, and the legacy of his writing and teaching made him a tower of strength in that turbulent and painful period as the new Church became established. And at a time also when the Jewish nation, under the oppression of Rome, would see its capital city and, with it, its magnificent temple, destroyed, and all the inhabitants driven out, just as Jesus had foretold would happen. It is difficult for us to realise how different our faith today would have been without what Paul has given to posterity.

Unfortunately, history reveals that the church, only some three hundred years later, would become embroiled with Rome through that nation's acceptance of Christianity as its state religion, inaugurated by the Emperor Constantine under the Edict of Milan in 313 AD. Then in 330 AD, Constantine 1st moved his capital from Rome to Constantinople. And then, as we can see from historical records, as the Roman Empire began to collapse in the 5th century due to decadence, a conflict of leadership, and the attacks of the Huns under Attila, it was the then Bishop of Rome, Leo I, who persuaded Attila the Hun in 452 AD not to sack the city. Christianity at the time was focused around five cities. Rome, Jerusalem, Antioch, Alexandria and Constantinople, each ruled by a Bishop. However, by 586 AD it was the Bishop of Rome who, by taking over the political and social structures of the Roman Empire where he exercised authority, became the dominant figure in the Church. Claiming as he did that Peter, given specific authority from Jesus, had lived and was martyred there, with the added suggestion that Paul had also been martyred there. He sought to benefit from the decline of political power and assume the vacant authority, which was ebbing away from the Roman Empire. But, by so doing, he made the Church become a political as well as a religious entity. A role it would sustain until relatively recently and one which, to many, seems completely incompatible with the life and teaching of Jesus. In the New Testament each church had an autonomous self-governing body, and any 'control' exercised was limited to guidance, instruction, and teaching. Either by letter, as from Paul, Peter and John in their epistles, or through scattered visits. But there was no settled authorial base, apart from the hometown of Jerusalem, which was the base for the ministries of Peter and James, our Lord's brother, as we read in the Acts. However, the role of Jerusalem would have been drastically reduced with the destruction of the city and the Temple by the Romans in AD 70, followed by the exile of all its inhabitants. Neither Jews nor Christians would return in any numbers for 2,000 years. Rome itself ceased to have any political or military significance by the 4th century. The Western Empire, in its closing days, was centred on Constantinople. So, Rome became the seat for the newly self-appointed Pope, or Father of the Church.

However, from our point of view as Christians, the significance of Paul's influence on the newly formed group of believers, who were first called 'Christians' at the provincial capital of Antioch, having previously been known as followers of 'The Way', cannot be overemphasised. Doctrinally, he is the father of our faith. Paul was first and foremost a very deeply committed religious believer. Born in Tarsus, a Roman city from which he derived his Roman citizenship, he had travelled to Jerusalem to study the Jewish faith as a Pharisee, the strictest of all the segments of Judaism. He possibly lived with his sister, whom we are told lived in Jerusalem. But it is not just his religious zeal which would have driven him. He abhorred the teaching of 'The Way' because it ran counter to his faith. Hence, his place at the stoning of Stephen and his solid persecution of any followers of The Way to the extent of obtaining letters of authority to seek them out in other cities. But from God's point of view, it was his deep knowledge of the Jewish Law which would enable him to see in it the symbolic references to the new faith and, after his conversion, to understand that this 'new faith' was not new at all but had been declared freely through all the symbolism of the Law and its teachings. So that one led directly into the other. The Gospel was the fulfilment of the Law, as he would later say, not the enemy of the Law, as he had initially thought. Romans 10:4

It was this 'conversion', begun so dramatically as he made his way to Damascus to destroy the New Faith, that convinced him of the truth about Jesus. Symbolically, he was made physically blind to convince him that what he then believed was a form of spiritual blindness so that when his physical sight returned, he would be spiritually restored into a true understanding of what God was doing. And that must have been an earth-shaking event for him.

However, for us, the most vital component of Paul's contribution to the Gospel is found in his letters, written to various churches but intended to be passed around and read. Here we have a detailed analysis of the basic concepts of the Christian faith, as Paul used his extensive knowledge of the Law to show us two things. First, the relevance of the symbolism of the very elaborate covenants which God had made. Beginning with the very simple ones made with Adam and with Noah, and then the much more detailed one made with Abraham. Here we have the first promise of a land and a nation, based on his, Abraham's own descendant, a singular noun, indicating the role of Jesus, as well as being based on his own children, through Isaac. Then we have the very extensive and detailed account given to Moses on Mt Sinai. Paul then, in his writings, identifies Jesus as the fulfilment of the Law so that Jesus becomes both our High Priest, perfect in knowledge and understanding, and, in His death, the sacrifice for our sin. Demonstrating how necessary these things detailed in the Old Testament had been in preparing the way for the truth about God's plan for His creation and in revealing how it would be fulfilled.

But there is so much more which we can learn from the history of the Jewish nation. How the history of Israel becomes a picture of the Christian experience, with its failures and its successes, showing how Israel failed to receive the fullness of God's promise to Abraham because of their disobedience and unbelief despite their knowledge of God's miraculous power. Whereas we, by believing in Christ and accepting forgiveness through His atoning death, can, if we are obedient to Him, become the children of God. Galatians 3:29 And if children, then heirs together of the Kingdom of God. Romans 8:17

Following his conversion, Paul immediately begins to preach in Damascus, but he is so effective in his arguments and so powerful in his delivery that a warrant is issued for his arrest. Fortunately, some of the new converts were able to help him to escape by lowering him secretly over the wall in a basket. But it is not just education which made Paul such an effective witness to Christ, demonstrated at his trial before both Felix and Festus, the Roman governors, where he had defeated all the Jewish opponents. We read that when King Agrippa came to Caesarea to visit Festus, it was Paul's account of his supernatural conversion which alarmed him most, not his arguments, and to avoid it he simply said, "Much learning has made you mad." Acts 26:24 Whereas in the case of the disciples after Pentecost, whilst the crowd version was that they were drunk (Acts 2:13), the conclusion from the local authorities, after hearing Peter and John speak with such power and authority, was that they "took knowledge of them that though they were simple and unlearned men, they had been with Jesus." Acts 4:13av. In other words, it was recognised that what was happening, which included in the case of the disciples, the healing of the man who had been lame from birth, was more than an ordinary human experience. The challenge for the church today is that so often it is seen as a purely human, but compassionate, organisation, but that does not reveal its supernatural, Holy Spirit-inspired origin; therefore, it does not glorify God. "Having a form of Godliness but denying the power thereof." 2 Timothy 3:5.

Leaving Damascus, Paul then goes directly to Jerusalem, which was at this time still the home of the Apostles and many of the disciples. However, with Paul's very recent persecution of the 'Followers of the Way', which had included the death of Stephen, at which Paul was present, they were terrified of him. It was at this point that he was taken in hand by a disciple named Barnabas from

Cyprus, also a new convert, who introduced him to the Apostles. However, Paul then began to preach and dispute with the Jews who denied the truth about Jesus, and they became enraged and publicly threatened to kill him. So, to avoid further problems, the disciples took him to Caesarea, and from there they sent him back to Tarsus, his home.

The next we hear of Paul was from Antioch. The Gospel had spread from Jerusalem to the Jews living there, as the new converts were scattered by the persecution which followed Stephen's death. But the Gospel there was being challenged by Gentiles, probably Greek-speaking. Barnabas, himself an early convert, who came from Cyprus and was probably Greek-speaking, was then sent there by the disciples from Jerusalem, which produced a very profitable mission. Barnabus then went off to Tarsus to bring Paul to join them, and it was from there, a year later, that the Holy Spirit called Paul (still called Saul) and Barnabus to begin their great missionary work. Taking John Mark with them, they set sail first for Cyprus and then into Macedonia, but whilst they were there, at Perga in Pamphylia, John Mark gave up and returned home. This meant that when they set off on the second journey, Paul refused to take Mark with them, and after a major dispute, they separated. Barnabas and Mark went back to Cyprus, whilst Paul took Silas back to Pamphylia. They were then joined by a very sincere and devout convert, Timothy, who joined them at Lystra, and they were also joined by Luke, the author of The Acts of the Apostles, when they left to obey the call for them to visit Macedonia, which Paul had received in a vision at Troas. We know that this is where Luke joins the group because at this point the narrative changes from referring to Paul's group in the 'third person', "they," and from now on Luke refers to the group as "we," obviously including himself.

Paul's three missionary journeys, described by Luke, end when he returns to Jerusalem with monies collected by the churches to help the poor Christians in Jerusalem. Whilst there, he is seen in the temple, performing a vow, and the Jews there became enraged, trying to kill him. He is rescued by a group of Roman soldiers, amazed when they hear that he is a Roman citizen. Summoned before the Jewish Council, the Sanhedrin, he preaches the Good News of Jesus, but the Jews, unable to defeat his message, plot to kill him. Forty men had sworn an oath, to kill him or die. Hearing of this, and because he was a Roman citizen, the Roman Commander sends Paul to Festus the Governor at Caesarea, escorted by a small army of men, comprising mounted and foot soldiers. Here Festus finds that as far as the law is concerned, no crime has been committed. But he allows the Jews to make their charges against Paul. We are then told that he is kept in custody for some four years, through the period of rule by both Festus and Felix, which included a visit from Agrippa and his wife. Altogether a remarkable opportunity for Paul to preach the Gospel to these men. Even Agrippa is powerfully moved by his message. Finally, they decree that, in fact, Paul has no case to answer, the issue raised having been a matter of Jewish belief, and so they would have released him. However, Paul was aware of the anger against him and realised that, if he was released from the custody of the Roman authorities, the Jews would kill him. So, in self-defence, he appealed to the emperor in Rome, which was his right as a Roman citizen.

Paul's journey to Rome, under guard, was an extremely perilous one, including a shipwreck, and took the best part of a year. On arrival there, he was kept under custody but was given a measure of liberty, and he had a great variety of companions during his years there. However, it became a marvellous opportunity for Paul to testify to his faith before the Court, Philippians 4:22, and, from our point of view, it was the time when Paul, writing to the various churches to instruct and guide them, produced for us that most comprehensive survey of our Christian faith, in what we call his epistles. Altogether, Paul's life was most remarkable, and, without his contribution, our understanding of the Christian faith would be much poorer. But what a cost to him personally. Luke's account of his life ends with Paul spending two years confined in Rome, from where he wrote so many of his letters to the churches and was visited by several of his friends and colleagues. We have no further news of him; Luke is silent. What I find intriguing is that Luke wrote his account of the early church and Paul's ministry, The Acts of the Apostles, after his last words about Paul spending two years in Rome. So, if Luke was alive and presumably still at liberty, why did he not continue writing about Paul? Had Paul died? Had Paul been set free and continued his ministry? Clearly, Luke himself was alive and free to write, but where was Paul?

Paul's Colleagues

Paul was such a committed individual that, on a personal level, he was unlikely to have been easy to live with, unless one shared his deep devotion to God and the service of Christ, whom, having not seen physically, he loved beyond measure.

We start with Barnabas because he had helped to get Paul accepted by the Apostles in Jerusalem and who, being from Cyprus, was possibly also Greek-speaking, as we know Paul himself was. Then it was he who sought Paul out in Tarsus to bring him to minister in Antioch and became his companion, chosen by the Holy Spirit, on that first preaching tour. What is difficult to accept was the "sharp argument" over John Mark, which led to them separating, Acts 15:39. Paul then took Silas with him, whilst Barnabas went off with his nephew Mark to Cyprus. Yet, later, we later hear of Mark being one of those who worked with Paul in prison, Philemon verse 24. But we hear no more of Barnabus.

Paul is then joined on his missionary journey by a young and deeply committed convert, Timothy. That Paul was close to him and confident in his ability is evident from the fact that he was left as pastor of the church in Ephesus, and he describes him in the first of two letters to him as "my true son in the faith," 1 Timothy 1:2. Ephesus was the city where the preaching of the Gospel had caused such controversy and a riot (Acts chapter 19), but the city had also proved very responsive to Paul's message (1 Corinthians 16:9). We also know, from Hebrews 13:23, that Timothy spent some time in prison and possibly also visited Paul in prison.

Luke, we have already met, because he was the writer of the Gospel in his name and the record of the early church, The Acts of the Apostles. However, we must not overlook his vital role as Paul's companion on his travels, including that disastrous shipwreck near Malta. Luke, who mentions both at the beginning of his Gospel and The Acts of the Apostles that he had been acting as a tutor to Theophilus, apparently the son of an official and whom he calls "Your Excellency", had apparently joined Paul at Troas and was certainly with him as a companion during his time in Rome. He would also have been an educated man and an ideal companion for Paul. Although doctors of his period had few of the skills or the knowledge of modern medicine, we must not write them off as ignorant. His medical skills may well have been the reason for him travelling with Paul.

Through the Epistles and as recorded by Luke in The Acts, quite a list of fellow workers and companions are listed. Priscilla and Aquilla, who, like Paul, were tent makers (Acts 18:1), met in Corinth and left in Ephesus, where they were subsequently joined by an eloquent speaker, Apollos. Priscilla and Aquilla met Apollos and found that, although he was a believer, he had only learnt the teaching of John the Baptist and that he was unaware of the coming of the Holy

Spirit. They pointed out that John the Baptist foretold that when Jesus came, He would baptise with water and with the Holy Spirit and fire. In fact, Jesus had specifically told the disciples NOT to go and preach until they had received this gift from His Father (Acts 1:4). For when He comes, He will convict of sin (John 16:8), lead you into all truth (John 16:2), and reveal the truth about God (John 14:17), and further, the coming of the Holy Spirit will convince them that He, Jesus, has successfully returned to His Father and that the Holy Spirit is His gift to the Church. Returning later to Ephesus, Acts 19: 1–7 Paul also finds that a group of twelve believers there had no knowledge of the Holy Spirit but only the baptism of John, the baptism of repentance. Paul then tells them about Jesus, and they too were baptised in the Holy Spirit.

Leaving there, Paul is joined in Achaia by a group of men, including Sopater from Berea, Aristarchus and Secundus from Thessalonica, Gaius from Derbe, Tychicus and Trophimus, Asia and Timothy – quite an international assembly – all confirming that Paul's ministry was having considerable success over a wide area.

Chapter 4
And Now the Future

What we know from scripture is that, whilst in the Old Testament, God only spoke to selected individuals and empowered them with His Spirit, as with Othniel in Judges 3:10 and Saul in 1 Samuel 10:9. In the New Testament the return of Christ to His Father meant that the Holy Spirit was given to the Church. As Joel 2:28 had foretold, "It shall come to pass in the last days that I will pour out My Spirit on all flesh." And it is the coming of the Holy Spirit on the Day of Pentecost which so radically empowered the early Church. Jesus, as recorded by John in chapter 14, verse 12, said, "Those that believe in Me will do what I do…yes, they will do even greater things." and: 16 "I will ask the Father, and He will give you another helper, who will stay with you forever. He is the Spirit who reveals the truth about God." Then, in John 16:4–17, we have further details of the work of the Holy Spirit. Surely it is the failure of the modern church to believe in and receive the power of the Holy Spirit which accounts for much of the modern decline in Christian faith. "Having a knowledge of the truth but denying the power thereof." 2 Timothy 3:5. The miraculous ministry of Christ began when the Holy Spirit came on Him at His baptism by John.

The interesting point here is that historically the Bible has no ending. After the record of The Acts of the Apostles, which concludes as we have seen with Paul still alive, we have then the section of letters, written by various church leaders, the most numerous being those from Paul. Apparently ending then with the remarkable series of visions given to the Apostle John, who had been imprisoned on the Isle of Patmos to stop him teaching and preaching about this new faith, originally called 'The Way'. By this time the name of this new faith had changed, and it was the group of believers in Antioch who were first called 'Christians', or followers of Christ, who was the founder of this 'new' faith. It is very important that we now consider several issues. One of which is that in the

165

New Testament there is no record of the Roman siege of Jerusalem, which lasted some three years, nor of the fall of the city under Titus, the son of the Emperor Vespasian and the destruction of the Temple built for them by their governor Herod. Nor is there any written record of the expulsion of the inhabitants. But the implication is therefore that either the Gospels and The Acts of the Apostles were written before AD 70, or that the details were so well known and recent that there was little point in recording them.

Most important is that, although the traditional Jews were bitterly opposed and did their level best to stop the spread of this 'new' faith, because it undermined their long-cherished beliefs, dating from their founding father, Abraham. The fact was, as Paul himself discovered and spent much of his time teaching, this was not 'new' but was clearly the rather startling fulfilment of those promises made to Abraham, and to which the many symbolic references were pointing. Looked at carefully, as Paul proceeded to do, Jesus was Great David's Greater Son. He was the one who was leading the Children of God, not to Canaan but to a greater future kingdom. As Paul would state, when Abraham left Ur, the Chaldean city, "He sought a city which hath foundations, whose builder and maker was God," not an earthly empire. Jesus, God's only son, was the real sacrifice, not Isaac. The great deliverance from Egypt was symbolic of humanity's deliverance from sin and death. As, symbolically, the serpent on the pole which delivered Israel from plague was Jesus, who said, "And I, if I be lifted up, will save all mankind from death." John 3:14. "The choice of Aaron to act as spokesman for Moses became a symbol of Christ's role as mediator between God and man, and the role of High Priest was a very limited version of the part Jesus would play. The High Priest, being mortal, was himself a sinner, and his length of service was restricted. Jesus is immortal and totally sin-free. He becomes the faithful High Priest, who is moved by the feelings of our infirmities, because He was in all points tempted like as we are yet without sin." He becomes, through His death and subsequent resurrection, both priest and victim.

Further, the coming of their new king, whose reign would never end, and the time when their nation would be the envy of the world had been foretold frequently by their prophets. Even to the details of His birth, as we commemorate at Christmas. The tragedy for the Jews was that they failed to recognise that Jesus of Nazareth had been born in Bethlehem, as prophesied. Neither did they understand that the power which enabled His miracles and gave Him such authority was all evidence of His Deity. And that the Jesus they delivered to Pilate to be crucified was the Son of God, the man born to be their King.

What we today must realise is that this Jesus told us that He will return (John 14:3), giving us some clear indicators as to when this will happen. As in Matthew 24:3–13, Mark 13: 3–7, and Luke 21:7–19. And the indications which He described are clearly to be seen here and now. Evident in the political scene with its threat of world conflict, in climate change and in the breakdown of social and moral standards. Jesus had warned His disciples, Matthew 24 and Luke 17, that after He had returned to His Father in Heaven, the troubles on earth would increase. But also, that the focus of world interest would increasingly turn to the Nation of Israel. As I write this, Israel is again fighting to preserve its integrity. Two thousand years have passed since the Romans destroyed Jerusalem and its temple and exiled its citizens. During that period and up until the present day, the Jews have continually been news. Persecuted by the nations where they found homes, it became an increasing issue, first in Russia with the Czarist Pogroms and culminating in their wholesale massacre in Germany during the 2nd World War. They finally retrieved their homeland in May 1948, only to find themselves immediately under attack from the Palestinian neighbours, and now, as I write, they are facing attack again from Arab and Islamic peoples. But what we know is that they, as the descendants of Abraham, are still the beneficiaries of God's promises to Abraham. And it means that we have quite considerable details of their future, outlined in the Bible and culminating when they will, "Look on Me whom they pierced." Zechariah 12:10, presumably at His return to earth. But note also the statement which precedes this: "And it shall come to pass in that day that I will seek to destroy all the nations that come against Jerusalem." Zechariah 12:9. Which can be seen as a warning to all nations against what is happening now.

We may also ask, "Will a nation be born in a day when Jesus returns?" Isaiah 66:8. Will Israel recognise Him then, as they failed to do two thousand years ago? And if so, what will their future be? Or is Paul saying that the future 'children of Israel' will be divided into those who have, like Paul, seen the error of their ways and become Christians and those who only at the point of His return see Him as their King? Paul's answer in Chapter 9 of his letter to the Roman church makes a statement in verse 6, "Not all the people of Israel are the people of God." And in verse 30 he says, "The Gentiles who were not trying to put themselves right with God were put right with Him through faith. while God's people, who were seeking a law that would put them right with God, did not find it. And why not? Because they did not depend on faith but on what they did."

However, in his letter to Romans, Chapter 11, Paul reaches a conclusion. Verse 1: "Did God reject His own people? Certainly not." And in verse 23 he says, "And if the Jews abandon their unbelief, they will be put back in the place where they were." And verse 25, "There is a secret truth…it is that the stubbornness of the people of Israel is not permanent but will only last until the complete number of Gentiles comes to God, and so all Israel shall be saved."

What we know about the future of Israel is that the promises of God made specifically to that nation have yet to be fulfilled. They were not fulfilled for Israel at His first coming, two thousand years ago. But Paul, himself a Jew but converted by Jesus to the Faith, is convinced that God will, at the right time, bring the Israelites to their senses. Which confirms that Israel as a nation will continue into the New Kingdom, though how and in what manner, we are not told.

Between the period of the Old Testament and the start of the New, we have a gap of some 450 years, filled in for us by historians. It is now two thousand years since the days of the New Testament ended, and the saga is not over either for the Jewish people or for us, because the promises given all those years ago to Abraham and passed on to his descendants were transferred to us when we, by our belief in Christ, became heirs together with them of the Covenant.

So, what does the future hold for the Jews and for humanity? What does Paul mean when he says, "I consider that what we suffer at this present time cannot be compared at all with the glory that is going to be revealed to us All of creation waits with eager longing for God to reveal His children. For creation was condemned to lose its purpose, not of its own will, but because God willed it to be so. Yet there was this hope that creation itself would one day be set free from its slavery to decay and would enjoy the glorious freedom of the children of God." Romans 8:18ff.

The Word of God is a gradual unfolding of His purposes, so that what God revealed to Paul is far more complex than what God revealed to Abraham and Moses. So, what about now, two thousand years after the time of Paul and the Apostles? Is there any further advance in knowledge and understanding? There should be. We have the promise of Jesus that when the Holy Spirit comes, He will lead us into all truth (John 16:12): "I have much more to tell you, but now it would be too much for you to bear. However, when the Spirit comes, He will lead you into all truth." The words of the New Testament, particularly in the Acts and the Epistles, are evidence that this did happen. But are we failing to receive further enlightenment because we are not responsive to the Holy Spirit? However, there is much in scripture which we can read and, with the help of the Holy Spirit, understand. It may be that the Word of God, as contained within the Scriptures, is the limit of what God is willing to tell us. However, when it comes to seeking to know exactly when Jesus will return, He admitted that even He did not know.

However, He did give His disciples some very useful guidelines, and He criticised His hearers for being able to read the weather but being unable to read the signs of the times. Whilst Paul can tell us some of the things which will happen after the Second Coming. For a start, he says in 1 Corinthians 7:31, "The world as it is will not last much longer." Now that may well be taken in the light of the current understanding of the age of the universe. What is equally certain is that God is outside of time. He is eternal, His name given to Moses, "I AM." Which translates as "I eternally exist," and phrases like "A Day with the Lord is as a thousand years and a thousand years as a day" 2 Peter 3:8. Equally, that we were "chosen in Christ from before the foundation of the world," and that the ultimate purpose of God is to "Bring all things together. Things both in heaven and on earth, with Christy as head."

We also know that "He has raised us up…to rule with Him in the heavenly world." Ephesians 2:6, which implies that when the existing heaven and earth 'dissolve in fervent heat' or are 'folded up like a garment', we shall enter the spiritual, eternal world, of which what is visible now is only a shadow. No wonder Paul said, "Eye hath not seen nor ear heard the things that God has prepared for them that love Him." And "If in this life only we have hope in Christ, we are of all men most miserable."

The one thing we must accept is that no one knows when Jesus will return. However, a belief in His return is widespread, extending beyond the Christian faith. Even Islam believes it. But what will happen when He comes? Most obviously, the first thing would have to be Judgement because of the behaviour of so many individuals and nations. God may be loving, but He is also righteous, just and 'holy', a God of order and justice. In the Old Testament, 'holy' frequently meant 'fire', physical or as a very bright light. But it also involved what was called 'worship', and that meant respect, humility, obedience, love, and a recognition of our status before God.

Where the Jews failed was in their belief that God's acceptance of them came from their own efforts, in keeping the Law and in their conduct. But this failed because human nature is biased towards promoting one's self. "What the Law could not do, because human nature was weak, God did." Romans 8:3. As illustrated in the story of Adam and Eve. And this is where the Christian faith is so radically different, because the Christian believer must come to realise that he cannot be justified in the sight of God through human effort. Salvation is the gift of God made possible through the death of His Son, who, by His total sacrifice, paid the penalty on our behalf. Galatians 1:4. Therefore, 'salvation' comes through believing that Jesus is God's Son and that God has accepted His death in payment for our sin and then living a life of worship in which we honour Jesus and obey Him. Galatians 2:16. At that point the failure of Adam is reversed by the obedience of Jesus, and by the action of God's Holy Spirit we are 'born again' as God's sons and daughters. John 3:16.

Now we get to the heart of God's plan for the future of the universe. For make no mistake, God is the creator of everything that exists, and everything was created for a purpose. The Bible states that the purpose of God is to bring all things in submission to His Son. Ephesians 1:10. And, as part of that, God has extinguished the difference between Jews and Gentiles who believe. They both become 'God's children and heirs together of the riches of Christ'. Ephesians 3:6. But, recorded as early as the time of King David, the scripture speaks, Psalm 96:13, of a time when the Lord will come to rule the earth with justice.

In some of His later parables, Jesus speaks of a King going away to receive a Kingdom, and when he goes away, He gives authority, or money, to his servants. Then on His return, He checks what they have done with the responsibility and rewards them with even greater authority, in accordance with their success in managing his affairs. Luke 12:41–48; Matthew 25:14–30. Which implies that the servants were being tested for their honesty and their ability. And it is possible that the same applies to our lives here on earth, that we too are being tested, possibly for greater responsibility in the future. But remember the threat made to the Hebrews in the wilderness, after yet another flagrant act of disobedience, that He would destroy the whole nation of Israel and begin again with Moses. Exodus 32:9. Obviously, they had failed to live up to the standard which He required. As had previously happened at the time of Noah, when God cleared the earth of all its inhabitants and began again with Noah and his three sons, Genesis 7. However, we know that there will be judgement when Jesus returns, because He said so, Matthew 25:31–46. And Paul repeats in 1 Cor 4:5, "Final judgement must wait until the Lord comes."

But what will happen to those whom He accepts as His children, those who, through belief in Him and in His sacrificial death, have been 'born again' as in John 3:16. These are the ones who are repeatedly referred to as "Chosen in Christ from before the foundation of the world." Remember that in the Old Testament God chose Jacob, the younger brother, and not Esau, who was by birth entitled to inherit, just as He had chosen Isaac in place of Ishmael, the elder son. They were chosen ultimately, like us, for, "An inheritance, incorruptible and undefiled, and that fadeth not away, reserved in heaven for you!" Peter 1:4. Paul also states in Romans 8:21. "There was the hope that one day creation would one day be set free from its slavery to decay and would share the glorious freedom of the 'children of God'."

"I proclaim God's hidden wisdom which He had chosen for our glory, even before the world was made." 1 Cor 2:7. Paul repeats, God "Gave us this grace before the beginning of time." 2 Timothy 1:9. And again in Titus 1:2. All implying that there is a glorious future ahead of us. What Christians sometimes forget is that Christianity as a faith is not designed solely for the benefit of humanity or the 'saved' person. We are the servants of God, here to do His bidding. So, in that sense, we exist to fulfil God's plan. But what is God's eternal purpose? Is it, as Paul says, "To fill the whole universe with His glory?" If John Milton, in his great poem 'Paradise Lost', written in the 17th century, is correct, God's original purpose for the universe was frustrated by the rebellion of Satan and his followers; then we will have to wait until they are all defeated and God's time is ripe, Revelation 14:15. Then God will take control. "Then the end will come; Christ will overcome all spiritual rulers, authorities and powers and will hand over the kingdom to God the Father. For Christ must rule until God defeats all enemies and puts them under His feet... But when all things have been placed under Christ's rule, then He Himself, the Son, will place Himself under God...and God will rule completely over all." 1 Corinthians 15:24–28. Then as joint heirs together with Christ, we shall share with Him the glories of the Kingdom of God.

The scripture says that we are, "Made in the likeness of God." Genesis 1:26 But "likeness" does not mean physical likeness; it means in character and personality. The resemblance is seen in the nature and character of Jesus. So we can say that "God is love" because Jesus was full of love. God is "holy and just, righteous and powerful," because Jesus exhibited these notable characteristics. In the same way, for us to be Christlike, we must exhibit the characteristics of Jesus' life on earth. But 'in the image of God' also means that we can communicate with God and respond to God. So that if we say that we 'love Him', it means that our human love is directed at Him. In the same way, we love the things that God loves. People are said to be 'incompatible' when they do not or cannot share the same things. Put very simply, we would not be happy in 'heaven' if we did not like what God likes. And that might rule out a lot of people. It does mean that we will share His objectives. On earth those objectives are directed to the benefit of humanity in such a way that humans can achieve the highest goals, which implies goals of righteousness and goodness. "Sin" is to fall short of the glory of God. Romans 3:23. Against this, the Bible describes historically the consequences of "sin."

The Bible is describing the purpose of God on earth, which is to bring the whole of creation under His control, the Kingdom of Righteousness. "That in the dispensation of the fullness of times, He might gather together in one all things in Christ. both which are in heaven, and which are on earth." Ephesians 1:10. Against which is ranged the whole regime of Satan, the forces of "principalities and powers, the rulers of the darkness of this world, the spiritual wickedness in high places." Ephesians 6:12. These forces, against which we are fighting here on earth, might well be active throughout the whole of the universe. "He gave Himself that He might deliver us from this present evil world." Galatians 1:4. It is possible that God has created humanity for the express purpose of demonstrating His love and His power, "That now unto the principalities and powers in heavenly places might be made known by the Church the manifold wisdom of God." Ephesians 3:10. It could be that He is also 'saving' men and women from sin, causing them to love and trust Him, testing them daily, in order that He might have servants who will go out to witness to the power of God, not just to the far corners of the earth, but also to the farthest corners of the universe. Because it is just possible that the evil forces acting upon this earth are also acting elsewhere. That would also explain why God has, to our knowledge, ended things and begun again at least once, as with Noah and the Flood, and then He rescued Israel from 430 years of captivity in Egypt only to threaten to 'end' them and begin again with Moses. All we can say with certainty is that in the Bible we have a record of a plan unfolding. Those events which occurred had in many cases been clearly foretold, as with the history of the nation of Israel. And therefore, we can expect that the projections for the future of that nation will also be fulfilled. They are still the children of God.

However, the New Testament introduces a new race of people, those who, by faith in the death and resurrection of Jesus Christ the Son of the living God, have been 'born again' spiritually. These people, irrespective of nationality, are not only the children of God, but they are also the joint heirs with Christ of the Kingdom of God, which implies the whole of the universe. All that is needed is for Jesus to return, as He promised, and finally defeat all the forces of evil, once and for all. See Revelation 20:11–21 and chapter 21:1–8.

Even so, 'Come, Lord Jesus'. Amen.